SECOND COLLECTION

SECOND COLLECTION

by JOEL WELLS

THE THOMAS MORE PRESS

Contents

"There will be a second collection...."
—*from the Roman Catholic liturgy.*

Memories of a Catholic Sexhood

INSPIRED by the current craze for both nostalgic confessions and candid sex tracts, I have decided to tell *all*. So that the reader can better locate himself, it should be noted that the author was born in 1930. He attended public kindergarten (a sexual wilderness), eight years of Catholic elementary school ("What's that in your lunchbox?"), four years at a Catholic high school for boys ("What's that in your locker?"), and four years at the University of Notre Dame ("What's that under your mattress?"). He then went immediately to three years of naval service which took him to such orgy areas as Newfoundland, the Dry Tortugas and Newport, Rhode Island.

At the end of all this he had not, strangely enough, become involved in either homosexual or bestial practices (the latter being difficult to engage in satisfactorily while at sea unless one is a terribly fine swimmer). In the final months he did tend to tremble visibly in those rare seconds he found himself in the presence of any female under sixty-five, but was sustained *virgo intactus* through it all thanks to the marvellous RC sexual code which had been, so to speak, both his rod and his staff. This teaching, the finer points of which are set forth below, will be largely incomprehensible to modern youth of any religious persuasion, but to Catholics over thirty-five it should bring back some memorable temptations and the means by which they were hurled back into the Devil's toolbox to the immense benefit of their immortal souls.*

A Catechism of Sex

Q. Why were you made?

A. To know God, to serve Him and to avoid the pitfalls of sex.

Q. What is the greatest commandment?

A. Thou shall not commit adultery—which means, of course, thou shall not fool around with sex of any kind. It is the greatest commandment because there are more ways you can sin against it than any of the others, and because all of these ways without exception are mortal.

Q. What is permitted to nonengaged Catholic couples?

A. Nothing. The question should not even arise since there should be no such thing as a non-engaged Catholic couple.

Q. What is permitted to engaged Catholic couples?

A. Hand-holding, exchange of fond glances and the occasional nonpassionate kiss.

Q. What is a passionate kiss?

A. For girls, one that would smear their lipstick; for boys, one that arouses concupiscence.

Q. What is concupiscence?

A. That which is aroused by passionate kissing, looking at dirty pictures in *Life* magazine and the like.

Q. How do you know when your concupiscence has been aroused?

A. It would arouse it if I told you.

Q. Is an aroused concupiscence always mortally sinful?

A. Yes, except when you are unconscious.

Q. If you are unconscious, how can you know that it's being aroused?

A. You will worry about it and feel guilty when you are conscious again.

Q. What is permitted to single Catholics who aren't engaged to anyone at the moment?

A. Nothing. This probably means that they have a vocation.

Q. What about masturbation?

A. You mean self-abuse or better yet, self-pollution. It is always mortally sinful. You must always confess it first and not try to slip it in casually between not saying your morning prayers and having uncharitable thoughts about your teacher. It is certainly the worst sin of all because it invites other temptations such as going to Communion on Sunday while in the state of mortal sin in consequence of knowing that if you stay behind in the pew while your parents and everyone else receive you will be marked for the dirty self-polluter that you are. The second great temptation is to risk your immortal soul by postponing going to Confession and perhaps polluting yourself again on the theory that it is no harder to say *twice* than *once*. This is hardness of the heart, of course, and must also be confessed. You must also remember to say whether you did it alone or with others.

Q. Why would you want to do it with others?

A. You might be a homosexual and it's important that the priest know this so that he can forgive you under the right category.

Q. What of dirty thoughts?

A. Impure or unchaste thoughts are always mortally sinful when they are not resisted. The fact that they will occur to you is not of itself sinful since we are the victims of original sin. But they must under no circumstances be entertained.

Q. How do you know when you've entertained them rather than resisted them?

A. There's no way to be sure.

Q. Which means?

A. That you have to keep track of them and confess them all as mortal to be on the safe side.

Q. What if you weren't sure and hadn't gone to confession and still wanted to go to Communion?

A. Quite literally, you'd be playing with fire. However, in such circumstances a perfect act of contrition might hold you over until the next Confession.

Q. How can you tell when you've made a perfect act of contrition?

A. When tears come to your eyes and you feel very certain that you're going to become a missionary.

Q. What about looking lustfully at members of the opposite sex, holding them firmly when you dance with them, and trying to grab them in the back seat of cars?

A. You know the answer to that!

Q. Well, what's permitted to validly married Catholic couples then?

A. Don't get smart! Hand-holding, passionate kissing, petting and even relief of concupiscence during fertile periods are all permitted to the Catholic couple, providing always that they keep their hearts open to the primary end of marriage which is the procreation of children.

Q. That's it?

A. What more could there possibly be?

* To complete the personal saga of the author's moral triumph: having survived intact to the age of twenty-three, he then married, fathered five children in seven years and found himself *virgo interruptus* at age twenty-nine. He has occupied the intervening years by jogging, reading Dale Francis and taking cold showers. He awaits the coming of the climacteric with bated breath and shriveled arms.

How to Make a Breakthrough in Vocation Recruiting Through Selective Advertising

Prefect
Congregation of the Priesthood
Vatican City

Your Eminence:

At the more or less direct suggestion of my Superior General, I am writing to explain about the vocation advertisement which I ran in *Playmate* magazine recently. He is of the opinion that you may already have encountered some of the resultant publicity.

I doubt that you have had occasion to become familiar with the magazine in question and I cannot include a copy for your inspection since it would be automatically destroyed by the Vatican Post Office. In my opinion it is a very fine periodical—for the most part—which contains articles and stories by some of the world's most renowned and respected writers. Unfortunately it also contains photographs of scantily clad young ladies, some of whom are "topless," as the idiom has it here, plus a regrettable few who are "bottomless," and a quite brazen one or two who are both, simultaneously. There are also a

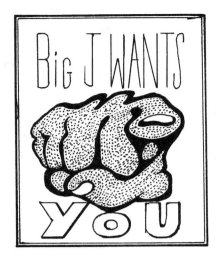

number of suggestive cartoons and drawings. In all candor I will have to admit that looking at *Playmate* is a directly proximate occasion of sin.

Why then, you may be asking—as did the Superior General upon learning that I had placed the ad—would one seek candidates for the celibate priesthood from such a readership? It's a fair question but irrelevant. For you must understand, Eminence, that statistics show *Playmate* to be the magazine most widely read by young men of all religious persuasions or lack thereof. Shocking as it may seem, it is as avidly perused on Catholic campuses as on secular ones. Thus I reasoned that if we were to rule out all young men who risked the proximate occasion of carnal sin by reading *Playmate* we would be cutting ourselves off from virtually all candidates.

Our own traditional campaigns in the Catholic press would seem to bear out this reasoning. Our standard advertisements in *Lily and Thorn, Boys of St. Bernard, The Chastity Crier, Offer It Up!* and *Custody of the Eyes* have brought in but four applications in the past seven years—one from an elderly gentleman in prison, two which were discarded because they came in scented envelopes, and one from a nine-year-old Congolese youth.

Our high school visitation program has fared no better. In many cases, the assembled students have laughed derisively at our veteran man in the field, Friar Ethelbert Mary, who always begins his talks with a prayer to our founder, Blessed Humperdink the Persistent. They make slingshots out of the elasticized waist scapulars he distributes and airplanes out of our three-color folder "Twenty-four Ejaculations for Personal Purity" (which don't come cheap, I can tell you). We've tried direct mailings to Catholic lads on their birthdays and sent Papal Blessings to their parents; we've offered free bus trips from metropolitan areas to our novitiate in Bismark, North Dakota (with free Cokes and potato chips en route); we've even promised plastic statuettes and Catholic art calendars to anyone who would write for one of our brochures—all to no avail.

Meanwhile, as I'm sure you must be aware, our order faces a personnel problem of crisis proportions. Aside from Brother Paul who suffers from chronic hiccups, I am the youngest member of the community—and I am forty-nine. Our median age has crept up to sixty-eight and more than two-thirds of our order now reside in the Humperdink Haven for the Bedridden. Bismark has three novices but doubts that two of them will last the winter. The Retreat Houses which have been our special mission are all in need of modernization—it seems that the soft, spineless retreatants we get today insist on central heating and indoor toilet facilities (cutting out tea and coffee at supper didn't work).

But it was when I phoned our major seminary in Dubuque and got no answer—the number had been disconnected—that I knew we were in real trouble. Radical action was demanded and I launched "Operation Breakthrough," as I like to think of it, forthwith.

The *Playmate* ad is only step one. I can't give you all the details and won't, because other recruitment directors who are in as much trouble as I am will copy them shamelessly. But I can say that you can look for some pretty unconventional and imaginative breakthroughs in the near future. Our stunning new "Swing with the Big J" posters are going up in selected singles bars across the country; the National Football League is considering my bid to sponsor the "Jesus Christ Super Bowl" on the Feast of the Circumcision; with the Vietnam war winding down I'm trying to interest Bob Hope in visiting foreign missions for his Christmas special next year; we're thinking of entering a Holy Ghost Turbine in the Indianapolis 500; Ara Parseghian has agreed to endorse our "Punt, Pass and Pray" competition; Dick Van Dyke will host our television series "The Vocation Game" starting next fall; and Mae West has done a series of color spots for us wearing a black mantilla and saying: "If I had it to do over again—and I do—I'd only confess to a Humperdinkian Friar."

I'm not at liberty to tell you exactly how many responses we've had from the *Playmate* ad. Suffice it to say that I'm already taking bids on the construction of a new wing for the Novitiate (with indoor pool, piano bar and sauna). And I can tell you something else—none of these new applicants used scented envelopes!

Yours respectfully in the all-new vineyard,

Chuck

Rev. Charles ("Studs") Winkler
Recruitment Director
Friars Regular of the Order
of Blessed Humperdink the Persistent

Cardboard Crosier
by Plimp Georgeton

WHEN my publisher Arnold Shameless first called to suggest that for my next book I "become" a Catholic bishop, I thought the dear old rascal had finally become dislodged from his tree. By this time I trust it's well-established that I'm no coward, but for a mere layman—not even a Catholic one at that —to undertake to infiltrate the Roman hierarchy was preposterous. I'd need a diocese, a limousine, a chancery office, episcopal ring and a course in fund-raising just for a start. And, without some degree of official cooperation or connivance, it would truly be mission impossible.

I had it in mind to dispose of this wild scheme quickly when I went up to Arnold's office and to offer my own alternative which was to become a Japanese Sumo wrestler. But no sooner than I'd put foot inside the room a voice shouted: "Stop right where you are, Plimp!" I found myself staring into the blinding rays of a spotlight which made it utterly impossible to make out Arnold, or indeed anything else in the office.

"That's him. What do you think?" I heard Arnold say conspiratorily.

A deep, slightly muffled voice replied: "Never do —way too skinny."

Could Arnold have possibly guessed my alternative proposal and rigged this mysterious confrontation to squelch it?

"There must be some *thin* bishops," I heard Arnold say.

"One or two, but they die young—no staying power."

The unknown voice carried a heavy freight of authority. Certainly, a man used to having his own way. Could I have under-estimated Arnold's knavery? Had the man actually succeeded in bribing a Catholic bishop into cooperating in this mad plan?

"All right, we'll pad him up a bit then," said Arnold. "Otherwise we'll proceed as agreed?"

"Mmmph!" said the stranger. "It's disgusting what we ex-bishops have to do to survive."

* * *

Three unbelievably arduous weeks later and I was being driven through the streets of Washington, D. C., in a long black Lincoln by a short Irish driver who threaded his way through the morning traffic with appropriate dignity. Dignity appropriate, that is, to the transporting of Bishop Terence O'Laughlin of Metro City, Texas, from his hotel suite to the Quarterly Meeting of the American Bishops. That was the name settled on me by former Bishop X who assured me that things were moving at such a frantic pace that no one would question my appointment and title on the simple grounds that they'd never heard of me or of Metro City, Texas. If questioned, I was to mumble something about a new population cluster around an ultra-secret space complex. My name would be entered illegally on the meeting roster and there would be a name-tag and manila folder just like all the others awaiting me.

My attire had been meticulously tailored and the gold chain which glittered diagonally down over my artificial paunch looked very official. I had learned to smoke thick Havana cigars without choking; I had memorized the names and faces of my fellow bishops, the Apostolic Delegate and a monsignor named George Higgins; I even had a small coat of arms stamped on the inside of my hat and on my attaché case—two anchovies rampant on a field of pizza to represent the prime tourist attraction of my titular see of Pepperoni.

The externals were all in order. What worried ex-Bishop X and what we had drilled and practiced into the small hours of the morning were the myriad

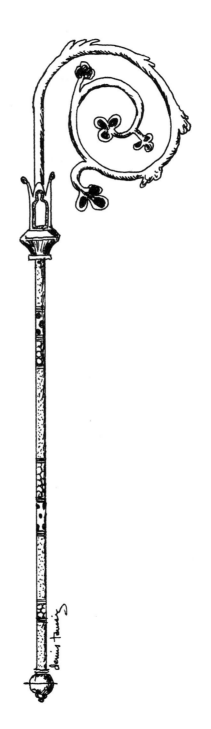

19

intangible details which could betray me in a second. Well, we would soon find out how well I'd mastered them. My immediate goal was to gain admittance to the morning's regular closed session—a feat accomplished by no laymen or member of the press in living memory.

The car pulled up under a canopy and I got out. The lobby of the Sheraton was jammed with reporters, priests, a group of nuns carrying signs which read "Sisters for Sex Education," and a dozen or so laymen who had knotted themselves into a group resembling a closed fist and were shouting obscenities at the trail of bishops who were beating their way upstream across the lobby toward the ballroom doors. I assumed a look of sublime indifference which I'd practiced in the mirror and plunged into the maelstrom.

"Good morning, Emmet," I said to the back of the head of a bishop whom I was suddenly thrust against. I'd had just a glance at his face and was pleased with the resultant instant recognition. He made an effort to identify me but the press was such that he couldn't manage even a glimpse. But the direct familiarity and the carefully honed timbre of my voice were sufficient to convince him that I was indeed a colleague. Bishop X knew his stuff!

"Isn't this disgusting," he threw back at me over his shoulder. "Those nuns should be back in the convent making hosts and I'd turn the fire hoses on that shouting rabble."

He gained another yard with me following his interference closely. (I was desperately afraid my paunch would become detached and move off to the side.) I almost betrayed myself by asking if such chaos prevailed at every meeting but caught myself in time to inquire in a bored tone if he expected anything interesting to come up at the meeting.

"Only the usual bunch of petitions from cry-baby priests," he responded throwing his hip into a porter carrying a heavy bag. "I did hear that security is tight this morning. Rumor is that some journalist is trying to crash the meeting."

"No!" I gasped, completely reverting to my own voice. Was it all going to be in vain? Had we been betrayed? By whom? Would I be fingered by ex-Bishop X as I approached the credentials table? Another example of the disgusting things "we ex-bishops have to do to survive"? Well, there was no turning back even if I wanted to. We were literally being funneled toward the doors of the ballroom.

Another few feet and I'd be in front of the table. As my line of vision cleared, I noted with horror that it was manned not by the harmless secretary I'd been led to expect, but by three fierce-looking prelates, two of whom I recognized as Cardinals. They were scowling and actually peering suspiciously into the face of each bishop as he freed himself from the mob, picked up his agenda and stepped into the calm of the inner sanctum.

Would they arrest me on the spot? I saw no policeman at hand. Then I remembered tales of the Spanish Inquisition and images of old Plimp being fed to the screw and rack began to surge up. At least Bishop X was nowhere to be seen.

Then Emmet made a final plunge which almost uprooted a potted palm (the Lions could use him at fullback) and broke into the clear. His movement was so sudden that I lost the shelter of his bulk and stood exposed before the table. But just then a man grabbed my arm—a reporter type with a portable tape recorder in his hand.

"Care to make a statement, bishop? How do you feel about admitting the press to these sessions? The people have an inalienable right to know!"

I felt the eyes of the guardian lions sweep over me like blowtorches. Then, as it so often does under fire, inspiration born of fear-flooding adrenalin came to me. I drew myself up to my full height and thrusting forth the hard amplitude of my plastic paunch, I turned on the reporter.

"I'm going to give you an inalienable right to the mouth if you don't let go of me and clear out of here. I wouldn't trust the press to cover a christening."

With that I turned back to the table, seized my agenda folder and strode into the ballroom under the suddenly approving eyes of the Cardinals.

"That's telling them!" said Emmet grasping my hand. "Come and sit by me, I like your style."

"For a big man, you don't move badly yourself, Emmet," I rejoined, clapping him on the back.

There were no more challenges. The meeting went off like clockwork and, of course, I'm not about to tell you peasants what went on.

What was truly amazing was the ease and speed with which the word got around. No letters, no posters, no rally, no ads. Yet somehow everyone was ready for the action when the great day dawned. Here is the merest sampling of what went on.

The Day the Over-Thirties Struck Back

8:40 A.M. Arthur Manchester, 54, dean of students at Chaos State University, leaves his office accompanied by six faculty members each of whom carries a sign reading: "This Is It!" They proceed single file across the campus to the Office of Records. Entering the office, they direct the personnel to line up against the wall. They then begin to remove the contents of file drawers containing undergraduate student credit transcripts. While a growing number of students gather, they carry the transcripts outside and dump them on the sidewalk in front of the building. When the last drawer has been emptied, Dean Manchester takes a Zippo cigarette lighter from the pocket of his coat, ignites it, holds it high above his head for all to see and then, smiling broadly, tosses it into the pile of paper.

* * *

9:15 A.M. Father Edward McGillicuddy, 63, pastor of St. Irwin the Inflexible Parish, vests for Mass in the sacristy, then strides into the sanctuary where he: (1) grabs the lay lector by the scruff of his neck and ejects him from the lectern at the right of the altar; (2) unplugs the thousand watt amplifier to which the choir's electric guitars are connected; (3) closes and locks the gates of the communion rail; (4) with the help of two specially recruited middle-aged servers, strips the low table set up in front of the long unused main altar and moves it to the side; whereupon two more servers appear carrying a life-size plaster statue (depicting St. Irwin in the act of castigating the Visigoths for riding their horses into St. Peter's Basilica) which is placed on the table; (5) announces to the congregation that all females without suitably long skirts and appropriate head coverings are to leave the church forthwith; and (6), turning his back on the people of God, approaches the steps of the altar,

makes the sign of the cross and in a loud, proud voice begins, "Introibo ad altare Dei. . . ."

* * *

9:20 A.M. Henry Farnsworth, 66, stops his 1973 Cadillac El Dorado at the traffic light three blocks south of his home. A red MG with straight exhaust driven by Harvey Ross, 18, pulls alongside, between Mr. Farnsworth and the curb. It is not Harvey's intention to make a right turn. As he has done on at least a dozen occasions in the past, it is Harvey's plan to pull ahead of Mr. Farnsworth as he crosses the intersection, leaving a suitable amount of exhaust smoke in his face before he reaches the spot where a car is parked some distance down the next block. The light changes but Mr. Farnsworth, unbeknownst to Harvey, has been watching for the appearance of the amber light on the cross-traffic signal. He has also shifted the El Dorado into low and now depresses the accelerator to the floor. Too late Harvey realizes that Mr. Farnsworth has somehow gotten the jump on him. Harvey tries valiantly to make up for lost time. The two cars streak across the intersection. But, alas, at that point where Harvey is accustomed to pulling to the left in front of Mr. Farnsworth, causing him to brake and drop back, he now sees only a substantial portion of right rear fender. It is Harvey who is forced to brake. But Harvey is unprepared and untrained in braking in such a situation. Nonetheless his quick young reflexes take command and he manages to stop the red MG almost, but not quite, before it makes contact with the car parked in his path. Only then does Harvey see that the parked car has a red light attached to its roof. Police Officer Curtis Tandy, 46, emerges from the parked car and waves his hand in the direction of the departing El Dorado. Then, walking with all deliberate speed, ticket book seated comfortably in his hand, he approaches Harvey.

* * *

10:15 A.M. Federal Judge Clayton Weatherspoon, 60, currently presiding over the 38th week of the trial of the Duluth Dozen, listens in the anteroom as his clerk calls for all present in the court to stand in anticipation of the judge's entrance. The defendants, following their usual custom, stand on their hands, on their chairs, on one another's shoulders—any and every way except with their two feet on the floor. Judge Weatherspoon, departing from *his* usual custom, does not mount the bench, but instead walks rapidly to the defendants' table. Pulling a large brown paper bag from beneath his robes, he solemnly presents each of the defendants with a banana.

* * *

11:45 A.M. The teachers of John Rawling's Consolidated High School move as a body to the student parking area and, breaking up into predesignated teams of two, let the air out of every tire on every car in the lot.

* * *

3:30 P.M. Chuck "Large-and-Loud" Lacey, 37, impressario of a three-hour radio program called "Scream Rock" locks the door of his sound studio from the inside and without a word of his usual snappy patter places the first of a tall stack of records on the turntable. It is the London Philharmonic's rendition of Prokofiev's "Concerto No. 1 for Piano and Orchestra."

* * *

7:55 P.M. Sheldon Fernglass, 43, father of two teenage daughters, emerges from the tool shed in his garage, slips quietly inside the back door of his house, moves through the kitchen into the hall where the eldest of his daughters is using the telephone to transmit to a friend the sound of a recording she has recently purchased. Mr. Fernglass opens the hedge clippers he has brought with him and, while his daughter screams, severs the phone cord with one snip. He then mounts the steps to the second floor, goes into his bedroom where he gathers up a book, pipe, pillow and dressing robe. He then proceeds to the bathroom, arriving there just a step ahead of his younger daughter who carries a large plastic bag filled with hair curlers. Mr. Fernglass bows, hands her the hedge clippers and goes into the bathroom, locking the door behind him.

* * *

11:30 P.M. Marjorie Hollaway, 39, mother of five, rises from the sofa and begins a tour of the eight rooms of her house. Using a flashlight she traverses stairs and bedrooms gathering up shoes, underwear, shirts, books, homework assignments, sweaters, trousers, coats—everything and anything that is not hung up or put away. Her husband turns on the outdoor lights and opens the front door for her. Together they go into the yard and distribute the various articles over lawn, hedge and bushes. Then, hand in hand, they go back inside and so to bed.

The Vatican Papers

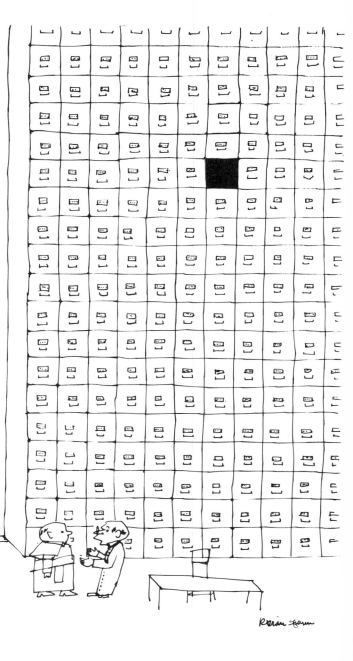

I. *Fragment of a letter postmarked Fatima, Portugal:* ". . . then in 1954 sell all GM and purchase Edsel; avoid a new issue called IBM; cigarette companies will boom in 60s; avoid entanglement in Common Market. . . . Convert gold supply to U.S. dollars in 1971. . . ."

II. *Memorandum dated 1962:* "Becoming increasingly clear that he intends to go through with dangerous Council notion. This must obviously be prevented at any cost. Direct assassination not only unchristian but out of the question, at least for the moment. I am seeing to it that the new 'doctor' urges him to eat more fatty foods to keep up his 'strength'. Also, that he decrease exercise. But the old man is apparently still strong as a horse which prompts O. to suggest a falling cornice during one of his garden promenades. B. rejects this as too obvious and, true to his lineage, suggests food poisoning instead. But I doubt that these peasants are susceptible. . . ."

III. *Letter to the Holy See dating from 16th century and signed simply,* "+Wolsey": ". . . The arrogant stand of More has rendered it verily impossible for me to grant openly the dispensation to Henry which his Holiness so generously placed in my power to bestow. If I now make publik the Writ of Annulment it will surely appear that More is holier than the Church herself and reaffirm his worth both with the impressionable Henry and the fickle common people. More is the slyest of serpents and would readily make it appear that I am susceptible to political ambition at the expense of the eternal verities of the Faith. As your excellency knows full well, my concern has never been for the staggering loss of revenues to myself (and proportionately to the Pence of Peter) which would attend upon Henry's rage should we deny him; rather, it has been for the terrible loss of grace to those souls in my charge who would be cut off from the sacramental bosom of Holy Mother Church if Henry chose to take this Kingdom out of communion with Rome. Thus, I have decided to withhold the Writ for the time being, risking the life of but one meddlesome layman. I do so in full confidence that Henry, having satisfied his lust for this toothsome wench called Anne, will contritely return to the fold and thus we will keep the Lion firmly within the provenance of the Holy See and this without sacrificing a single coin."

IV. *Position paper dated 1966:* "Our final consensus is then unanimous: the Encyclical should be issued forthwith. There will be a tiny and brief outcry from dissident factions, principally in the United States of America and in the Netherlands, but the majority of the faithful will welcome the benign words of the letter with joy and gratitude as a balm upon the troubled and aching wound of their consciences. The unfortunate publicity given in the world press to the spurious findings of the special commission (that leak has been attended to, by the way, with the recent creation of the diocese of Tierra del Fuego) will be successfully countered by our well-sown hints that artificial contraception—'the pill'—is a Communist plot to bring the White Western world to an enervating zero population growth while Red China, Black Africa, Brown India and the Atheistic Russians triple their populations with the aid of drugs designed to induce multiple births. This is quite true, of course, and need only be made public.

"Bishop W assures us that he can handle the United States with ease, the press being, as he puts it, 'in the palm of my hand.' (W, by the way, should be at the top of the promotion list; he would welcome the chance to come home to the Eternal City; however, he does bear watching, in our opinion, as he is fully capable of dreaming the impossible dream.) Best of all, the encyclical will crystallize and re-establish papal authority and the sovereign rule of the magisterium at the expense and ultimate overthrow of the insidiously democratic heresy of collegiality."

V. *Unclassifiable fragment, 1971:* "It has come to the attention of this august office and, indeed, to the personal attention of the head of this office, that the very explicit *no-no proprio* which we issued only three hundred and twelve years ago this month is being totally ignored. For the benefit of those with ephemeral memories, that paper was entitled *In Flagrante Delicto* and it set specific guidelines as to the amount of female flesh which could licitly be exposed within the confines of Vatican City— namely, the nose, fingers and hand (to the middle of the palm), the chin and (bowing to the pressure of fashion) the mouth.

"But what do we find now? Vast exposures of wrist, forearm and even shoulder; toes, ankles, calf, knees and—I must be frank—glimpses of thigh! Then, only two years ago, numbers of American and English females began to attempt to enter the Basilica itself in a wisp of cloth which our agents ascertained to be called the 'mini skirt.' This onslaught caused several of our veteran flesh-checkers to suffer fatal seizures (two remain mysteriously unaccounted for). But those who survived took comfort in the knowledge that the Devil, having raised skirts as far as it was physically possible to do so, would now turn away in shame-faced defeat. Who

could have imagined that there was anything more?

"I will not play into the Tempter's hands and describe 'hot pants' to you. In the words of St. Paul: 'The eye hath not seen. . . .' Suffice it to say that our checkers' measuring devices were of insufficient scale to record the amount of above-the-knee transgressions committed. To attempt even a rough estimate was to risk the direct occasion of serious mortal sin.

"This office is all the more appreciative, then, of the admirable and selfless zeal of the many who have recently presented themselves as volunteer checkers. But we have word that the worst is still to come: something called the 'bra-less look' and the 'pants suit.' Both of these abominations are sponsored by an international band of harlots calling themselves 'Women's Lib,' who are even now planning fresh assaults of concupiscence. We shall not fall into their wanton trap. Henceforward, each and every female who seeks admittance to the Vatican should be stopped at the gates and required to don a full-length black cassock. Females will then resemble, with but two regrettable differences, our fellow priests."

Massacre of the Innocents

(A Trauma in One Act)

Setting: a contemporary urban Catholic home. Father, mother and their four children are just sitting down to dinner. The children range in age from six to thirteen—two boys and two girls. They are dressed in the uniforms prescribed by the parochial school which they all attend.

FATHER (*crossing himself*): Bless us O Lord and these Thy gifts which we are about to receive from Thy bounty through Christ our Lord. Amen. In the name of the Father and the Son and the Holy Ghost. Amen.

MOTHER (*severely*): What's the matter with you children? None of you joined in with dad or even made the sign of the cross.

(*Silence*)

FATHER: Somebody had better give us an answer—Michael?

MICHAEL (13): It's a square prayer, that's all. And nobody's said Holy Ghost for years.

FATHER: Listen, buddy, if I want to say Holy Ghost, I'll say Holy Ghost. Is that what they teach you in Catholic schools these days—to call your parents square? If my grace is so bad let's hear one of you guys come up with something better.

PETER (6): Rub-a-dub-dub, thanks for the grub. Yeah God!

FATHER: My Lord, Agnes, did you hear that? What's going on over at that school? Peter, just where exactly did you learn that . . . that jingle?

PETER: In religion class—we made it up. Miss O'Malley said it was great.

FATHER: And who, for the sweet love of Mary, is Miss O'Malley?

LAURA (10): She's our Coordinator of Religious Formation and Christian Life Experience.

FATHER: Your which of what? Don't the sisters teach you religion? What about the priests?

MOTHER: I'm afraid none of the children are taught by the sisters this year, Fred. There are only two left—the principal and the music teacher. The priests spend most of the time downtown with the adopted parish or at the public high school counseling.

SALLY (12): Only one sister now, mom. Sister Yvette left yesterday. She got a leave of absence to form her own rock group—the Novice Mistresses.

FATHER: You can't have a Catholic school with only one nun and a bunch of hippy priests. What's the good of my forking out all that tuition if it isn't a Catholic school in the first place? You can see more nuns in our department store than at the school, any day of the week.

MICHAEL: You're missing the point, dad. We're not interested in having a Catholic school with a big "c." Miss O'Malley says it's time we outgrew the ghetto mentality and learned to think of ourselves as Christian activists in the broader context of contemporary society. Commandments, dogmas and rote catechism answers don't make you a Christian, just a member of the Roman Catholic cult. At our school we're involved in creating a microcosm of future community.

FATHER: Sacred Name of Jesus, will you get that! Meet the everloving press! I've never heard such a line of patter in my life—a regular John Cameron Swayze of the dinner table. This O'Malley woman is dangerous, Agnes. Does Monsignor know what's going on in those classrooms?

PETER: What's a Swayze?

SALLY: A man who used to tie wrist watches to skis on TV in the olden days. Dad means that Michael sounds too glibly articulate to be speaking authentically.

PETER: Oh, I see.

FATHER: My God, the rot really runs deep! I never actually knew what they meant by original sin until now—it's built into them. The devil knows his business. Adam, Eve and now my four kids.

LAURA: You mean our mythical first parents? We know now that Genesis was just a convenient way of accounting for creation to prescientific, pretheological people who didn't know about evolution. They were all hung up on the problem of how to account for evil in a world supposedly run by the direct will of an all-good God. So they had to personify evil in the person of the Devil and make it kind of genetically transferable in the notion of original sin.

FATHER: Jesus, Mary and Joseph! They've even gotten to you.

MOTHER: Don't swear in front of the children, Fred. I don't know what you're getting so worked up about. They still go to Communion every Sunday.

FATHER: Children? Children? They sound more like post-graduate draft-dodgers to me. I doubt that I know any swear words they haven't heard. And I'd be interested to know what they believe about Communion. Is it still the body and blood of Christ or some kind of inner-city snack these days. What does Chairman O'Malley tell you about that?

MICHAEL: With your hostile attitude, dad, I don't see much point in attempting a serious dialogue.

SALLY: Michael's right. You're not showing any respect for us as individual members of the pilgrim church trying to find our path through the darkness of authoritarian and parental oppression.

MOTHER: Sally, I'm not at all sure what that means but it sounds very disrespectful to me. And Michael, if you know what's good for you you'll answer your father.

MICHAEL: Well, since Vatican II, theologians have realized that the traditional concept of transubstantiation is inadequate and is turning off an awful lot of people. I mean, how far can you get by insisting that essential accidents are only appearances. We do a lot better by framing the mystery in terms of transignification. . . .

FATHER: I knew it! Another 10-syllable heresy.

MICHEAL: See mom, I told you it's no use. . . .

LAURA: What's wrong with pretending that Jesus is really in the host?

MOTHER: Laura, you know better than that.

LAURA: Yes, but I still like to pretend.

FATHER (*choking*): That does it—we're taking them out of school tomorrow.

LAURA: Please don't do that, dad. We like it at Saint Christopher's even if such a saint never existed. And besides, we're just getting to the best part of our sex education course—Genital Anxieties and How to Handle Them.

MOTHER: Leave the table, Laura!

PETER: I thought you weren't supposed to handle. . . .

FATHER (*pushing back his chair wildly*): Not supposed to what?

MOTHER: Don't ask any more questions, Fred. Please don't ask any more questions.

I Will Make Water in the Desert

NEARLY everyone will agree that the new three-year cycle of scripture readings for the liturgy is a grand idea. But as the newly translated Old Testament passages and their accompanying responsory verses come round, quite a few people find it difficult to understand or relate to the words and images in a very meaningful way.

These troubled people would, I'm sure, be the first to admit that it is their own woeful ignorance which prevents them from appreciating the intricacies of ancient Jewish history and culture. It is hardly the prophet Hosea's fault, for instance, that most people don't know what he meant when he has the Lord say: "How could I treat you like Admah, or deal with you like Zeboiim?" If the people of God did comprehend Hosea's meaning, they would see at once how fitting it is that their response to this reading is: "You will draw water joyfully from the springs of salvation." As it stands, however, most people just shake their heads and mumble something unintelligible.

Realizing that most people are caught up in the superficialities of modern life, it is deplorable but perhaps understandable that churchfuls of people, anxiously waiting to rush their families to the nearest pancake house after Sunday Mass, are going to be less than enthusiastic in chanting, "To the upright I will show the saving power of God," as a response to the verse that asks "If I were hungry, I should not tell you. Do I eat the flesh of bulls, or drink goats' blood?"

For a while vernacularists hoped that the fresh new translation of the bible would be sufficient to overcome the culture gap. Thus, when the woman in the parable finds the *dime* she had lost, she calls in all the neighbors to celebrate with her. Obviously, that makes more sense than having her find a drachma or a melchizedek, or some other forgotten ancient coin. But evidently it hasn't worked out as planned. Now may be the time for the liturgists to face up to the fact that contemporary Catholics are invincibly ignorant of and indifferent to the Old Testament—in any conventional translation.

What I'm proposing here is that the Old Testament readings be rewritten to incorporate contemporary images capable of penetrating the modern consciousness. The new versions would have to be compiled with great sensitivity and, of course, should vary from nation to nation. Americans, for instance, are not moved by the news that "the angel of the Lord struck down in a single night 185,000 Assyrians." Who cares about Assyrians, anyway? But make them Viet Cong or possibly Red Chinese and you might get an enthusiastic response like, "Smite them with your right hand, oh Lord." In Russia, China and Cuba, of course, it would be the Americans who get smote.

Understandably, the job of rewriting the entire Old Testament is too large for me. In the sample which follows I merely wish to indicate the approach, tone and level of banality which must be realized if we are to drive home the full meaning of the Old Testament to the mentally impoverished citizens of the global village.

READING

Then the atheistic communist Pharaoh sent for the president of the People of God and told him: "Moses, your people had better pray to that so-called god of theirs as hard as they can because I'm going to raise income taxes, personal property taxes and real estate taxes; I'm going to bus their kids to a different school every week; I'm going to distribute nothing but X-rated films to their neighborhood theaters and build low-income housing in their parks; I'm going to raise the price of meat, canned goods and milk and see that everything is sweetened with cyclamates and fried in saturated fat. I'm going to have motorcycle gangs ride past their churches during services and cause the garbage pick-ups to be cut in half. And, oh yes, there will be nothing but pay TV. All this and more I'm prepared to inflict upon them. But I'll call the whole thing off and give them an extra paid holiday every year if only they forget about this silly Yahweh of theirs, admit that I'm the greatest and only God, and write a few psalms, novels and technicolor movies about me."

To which Moses replied: "There's no way, wicked communist Pharaoh, to make my people turn away from their God and worship you. Furthermore, if you attempt to do any of the things you threaten, Yahweh is going to rip you off ten ways at once. In fact, he's going to do it anyhow if you don't let my people go."

RESPONSORIAL PSALM

LECTOR: The wicked one threatened us with terrible things, with cruelties and hardships past all bearing.

PEOPLE: Sock it to him, Yahweh!

LECTOR: But Moses told him where to get off;
That we would be steadfast and true.

PEOPLE: Fill his yard with crabgrass, Yahweh!

LECTOR: To you alone will we sing song;
To your voice only shall Charlton Heston hark.

PEOPLE: Clog his septic tank, oh Yahweh,
Jam his overhead door,
And if he tries to fight us
Give him hepatitis.
Alleluia! Alleluia!

Survival Manual for Fathers

WHILE reams of misty-eyed articles have been written about the sad lot of the surburban mother (St. Joan of the Station Wagon, martyr to the perpetual motion of her offspring), nothing but canards have been spread on dear old dad. He is the heavy in the Women's Lib scenario—the blithe begetter, the martini-swilling drive-in lothario who gets his kicks on the weekend and then disappears back into the bliss of executive chauvinist pigland waving his *Wall Street Journal* as he boards the air-conditioned 8:15.

Suburban fathers know this is vicious rubbish. If, till now, they have chosen not to challenge the image it is only because the truth reveals them to be such pitiful creatures, steers with brass rings in their noses which are removed only when they are required to pay through them.

This is a call to revolution. Fathers of suburbia, you have nothing to lose but your conformity. Throw off the chains of nice-guyness, of dutiful dad, of hero of the United Fund, of Scouter of the Year, Pillar of the Parish, of Tireless Champion of Kiddy Sports and Culture.

The following manual of guerrilla tactics has been prepared and tested by a veteran-dad who offers it with open hands to all fathers who are more than ready to stop playing horsey to Lady Godiva and the Seven Dwarfs.

1. Scouts

Cubs, Brownies, Campfire Girls, Boy Scouts, etc., are great for kids and bad for dads. Their pitch never varies and is deadly: "If you want your child to get the most out of the program, you've got to participate personally." The basic tactic to employ here is the creation of a credible image of total irresponsibility. *Do* go to the New Dads' Get-Together smelling of beer. Do *not* rise during the Pledge of Allegiance. *Do* smoke a cigar through the prayer to the Great Webalo or whatever. *Do* single out the head man or woman and tell them a filthy joke (the one about the Brownie Fly-Up is always good). This should be enough, but if they persist in phoning you to drive a dozen or so kids to Manitoba for the weekend overnight tell them that you'd love to but you've let your insurance lapse and your license has been revoked for drunken driving.

(There is a special hazard called "The Pinewood Derby" in which father and son are supposed to hack some semblance of a racing car from a block of impossibly hard wood and then roll it down a little ramp in elimination heats that go on for months. You have to watch out because some kids are surprisingly good with their hands and will carve out a winner in spite of you. If it appears that the car will move at all the only thing to do is secretly crimp the axle immediately before the first race.)

2. The Whole School Scene

This is tougher to deal with because your wife will bring all sorts of domestic pressures to bear, but it must be handled firmly or you can suffer losses capable of wiping out all gains in other areas. Repeated belching at the PTA mixer is good for a start. Laughing loudly and derisively at the end of the treasurer's report comes next, followed by an overtly clumsy effort to pour a quart of vodka into the punch. Ogling a few of the younger teachers is excellent; also holding onto their hands and squeezing their elbows after introductions. In the unlikely event that your wife asks you to go to another meeting with her, simply tuck a lightly rolled copy of *Screw* in your jacket pocket.

The annual round of parent-teacher conferences on the progress of your children are painful experiences to be avoided at all costs short of self-mutilation. They are hard on your ego, as well, since the teacher sadistically reads off a well-documented list of failings and felonies which add up to a general indictment of your child for moral and mental turpitude. "Does Johnny start a lot of fires at home, too?" is the way they usually begin. The teacher will then glance at you in a way which makes it very clear whom she thinks the kid takes after.

Wives are especially sticky about wanting your company at these little crucifixions. It's therefore imperative to say: Yes, by all means you'll be there, you wouldn't think of copping out on something so absolutely essential and therapeutic. This will lull her into a false sense of tranquility and she will make a definite schedule of meeting times that cannot be changed. Next you must find & memorize these times (experienced wives will not let you have this information until you are caught helplessly at home) so that you can call from somewhere at the last possible moment and say that you've been mugged. This ploy has the added benefit of accounting for the money missing in consequence of your free night on the town.

3. The Sports Mess

The wise father will ridicule all sports as a matter of principle. Inevitably, however, some boys will not be deterred from Little League, foot and basketball teams, hockey, track and the like. This is going to cost you a good deal of money but it need not cost you valuable hours as well, *if* your aspiring athlete knows from the very beginning that dad is going to be a source of embarrassment to him. This is easily accomplished by going to the first game, sitting up close where the coach and all "the guys" can hear you yelling things like, "Stout swinging, Snodgrass!" whenever Kelly or Murphy get a hit. Use words like, "chaps," and "jolly good" and "smashingly well-played." Nobody will tell you when the next game is scheduled.

4. Charities, Petitions, Community Involvement

When asked to be neighborhood or block captain of any drive you must say very quickly that your parole officer forbids you to handle any funds.

When asked to take up a petition or to attend a rally respond simply that your religion forbids terrestrial entanglements.

It is no longer safe to tell door-to-door collectors that you gave at the office because some of the slicker drives are beginning to cross-check names with computers. To all appeals for disease-alleviating funds it is far better to stagger a bit in the doorway and say that you are, unfortunately, a victim of the very malady in question.

Finally, all worthy cookie and candy sellers are quickly turned aside by the disclosure that your whole family is diabetic.

Chicago and Miami and Beyond

(N*rm*n M**L*r Covers Genesis)

AS NO reader of the mass media can possibly fail to know, your reporter is paid to experience things for them. He is no stranger to raw feeling, to naked sensations that would simmer their WASP hearts in adrenalin. As these same magazine readers could not help but discover in those several golden years when the reporter's pugilistically Edwardian face peered accusingly at them in half-rolled distortion beneath the eagle on their mailboxes, he was indeed the archangel of all American experience. The reporter got out, and around and into life while they stayed safely at home, risking no distance so great that they might be picked off by one of fate's sudden lefthanded throws toward the television set or the frostfree refrigerator.

They left it to the reporter to march for them, to campaign up and down the dangerous midnight streets of Gotham City while law and order took a shower in Scarsdale; left it to him to punch the bully in the mouth, to love and howl, talk and write about it all for them. They would try their own hand at drinking, but never joyfully as did the reporter, who knew how to pour it straight from the bottle without measuring it in the jigger of guilt. My God, he even had to stop smoking for them!

All this simply by way of establishing that gut reactions were mother's milk for the reporter. The reader will appreciate, then, that when he says the *greatest* experience he ever had was simply coming into being on that day without hours when God, or Howard Hughes, or somebody with considerable technical know-how, created the universe—when *he* says it was something else, we're not talking about the gaspy sort of little thrill that *you* get on the morning you discover that the $3.98 bag of Scott's really has killed off the dandelions.

Orgasmic awareness first of all; something palely akin to being socket, bulb and red-hot filament in a lamp switched on in an unknown room; or perhaps being John Updike. There was the whole unblinking show—sun, moon, stars and earth where but the second before there had been nothing, or at least no writer with the awareness to appreciate them. Your reporter readily admits it: he was impressed, impressed to the point of vertigo.

For a star-struck instant, he would confess to a political running-mate late one night many years afterwards, he felt that perhaps, just perhaps, it was he that was making it all happen. To which the running-mate, with theological astuteness not frequently exercised, replied that it was just possible the reporter had committed original sin. Subsequent events turning out the way they have, the reporter was just as happy not to have to take credit for them.

What had happened, in fact, was that the reporter's ego had come into being simultaneously with the outflooding of his primeval awareness, and the mildly dizzying effect he had experienced was simply a consequence of this giant force rushing out to fill the limits of the void. And there were limits, he was quick to sense. For one thing, his awareness, preternatural as it was (and is and always shall be, words without end), nonetheless seemed compelled toward that single planet which Richard Milhouse Nixon was later, on a droll little signpost planted in the surface of the moon, to so happily call Earth. Things were happening down there and apparently nowhere else. The reporter's nascent eye, which so many angels were to assure him resembled the luminous blue of the planet's then still surging waters, was quick to spot the action.

Evolution played its hand with agonizing slowness, pondering the simplest move like Adlai Stevenson deciding whether or not to run. Things began to stir about in the oceans and presently, in a variety of unsavory forms, to emerge and crawl about the land. Endless and bloody thrashings later there came mammals, sex, and finally a pair of naked hippies— flower children making love in the shade of giant ferns—who actually seemed to be having sensations for themselves.

The reporter, never one to beat a dead myth, sensed that his job was done and went out for a richly deserved drink. Things were on the right track and nothing could go wrong. While he was out of course, the hippies took some bad advice and blew the whole thing.

The rest is history—inexorable folly pursuing the Bitch Goddess down the centuries only to end up panting and ankle deep in the filth of the barnyard of the present.

Still, the reporter took understandable pride in the knowledge that it was he who had been singled out to cover the story. He couldn't, for all his carefully cultivated lack of hubris, quibble with the choice. His was, after all, the most versatile and pulsing pen in all the West (to tell but half the truth). He should have been warned—should have taken some lesson from the carnage of the great lizards, from the wanton twinkling of the painted toenails of the Bitch Goddess herself. In that other extant report of creation, the strictly hearsay account pieced together by desk-men from various wireservice accounts, he recalled, too late, a stuffy aphorism to the effect that "pride, goeth before the fall."

It had not been his alone. The cosmos, like a sneaky TV network, lacked the basic faith to trust the event to one well-focussed and articulate pair of camera eyes. The reader, who by this time may be glancing nervously at his watch, is asked to imagine only one more thing: the reporter's trauma when he learned, purely by chance and an anonymous phone call, that somewhere else, on some teak-paneled, red-carpeted cloud nine, Buckley and Vidal had been providing a running commentary of the same event.

I Am a Married Catholic,   I Want to Be

BECAUSE they have never really understood me or my innermost needs, what I am about to write may be resented somewhat by my wife and five children. They may find it difficult to believe that I am not motivated by spite or selfishness, but by the deepest anguish and utterly open-hearted love. But I am through with hypocrisy and sham. The truth is that I am tired of being married, tired of being a father, and that I want desperately to become a priest.

But my desperation means nothing to society or the Church. I am caught in an age-old trap from which there is no escape. At thirty-seven I am hopelessly cut off from any hope of ever realizing my ambition. The Church will never know what it's missing—the great building drives I might have pushed over the top, the stirring homilies I might have preached, the brilliant light and wisdom I might have shed on these troubled times—all of me wasted, turned back in on myself, poured back down the drain of my own enormous potential.

My heart sinks when I think how many times single people have approached me hoping for an open and positive response to their tortured pleas to join them in a game of poker, golf, tennis, or simply a convivial afterwork beer, only to be turned heartlessly aside by the only answer I can give—the only answer the system allows me to make: "Sorry, the wife's expecting me." How many times have these hands of mine which yearn to hold chalice and breviary instead been immersed in dish water or the icy depths of a clogged toilet bowl.

I could go on and on with such questions but I don't want to break your heart. Nor do I fancy that I am the only man trapped by the system. I am confident that I speak for thousands of married Catholic

a Priest

men whose tongues are muted by conformity and fear of "the little woman." Let me tell you the brutal truth about our lot.

Our days are spent in an endless and humiliating scramble for the dollars necessary to feed, clothe, house, educate and entertain the great brood of children we have spawned. Our evenings are consumed as a sacrifice to the insatiable maw of "close family relationships" of an intensely "I-Thou" nature such as bickering, helping with homework, taking out the garbage and paying bills.

Our much envied suburban weekends are twaddled away fixing broken windows and bikes, cutting grass, washing the rusty, rattle-ridden station wagon, and applying Band-Aids to filthy juvenile extremities while our wives rush forth on wanton shopping sprees for such luxuries as roach powder, Sani-Flush, hair spray and Lavoris (my toothpaste bill alone would keep a celibate in liquor—good liquor—for a year). While the children amuse themselves disjointing the plumbing, the repairmen come and go in sports cars paid for by the conspiratorial malfunctioning of the many ingenious appliances needed to run up my electric bill to a suitably staggering monthly total.

When my wife finally returns because her charge

cards have overheated, and the children have devoured fourteen hamburgers, been hosed down and bullied off to bed, we settle down for the legendary moment known as "domestic bliss." This consists of watching the late show on our pre-Edison model television set while indulging ourselves shamelessly with a six-pack of beer purchased in lieu of the new necktie I need. All of which is prelude to that which, for which, on account of which this whole banal life-drama is enacted—the sacred mystery of conjugal sex. Being a Catholic, of course, the unspeakable joys of this union are somewhat dimmed by the ever-present fear that my wife, whom nature has seemingly endowed with the ability to get pregnant simply by walking through a field of poppies, may conceive yet another proof and tribute to the primary end of marriage.

You will understand, then, why I yearn for the dignified, calm, and infinitely rewarding life of a priest. In addition to the spiritual stature which is automatically conferred, I yearn for those quiet evenings in the rectory, those golden hours spent in the confessional guiding and uplifting the lives of people like myself. And if, perchance, a problem or doubt should cloud the sky of priestly tranquillity, it is only necessary to turn to the wise and kindly pastor for help and warm, paternal counsel.

Not for the priest the eternal and frenetic quest for dollars; not for him the soul-shrinking breakfast full of sound, fury and flying cereal. Rather, he can take comfort in the mature delights of evening walks about the parish, of stimulating conversations with his fellow priests, of a weekly round of golf, of winter vacations to Florida, of an occasional commendation from the Bishop—these are but a few of the things a priest can count on, the very things I yearn for and will never know.

There will be those, I suppose, who will mistake my anguish for envy. There will be those, too, who will say that I have oversimplified and exaggerated my case in order to make my point. It is always thus when a man dares to lay bare his soul. I can only hope and pray that the Church will heed my honest searching, and move to relax its rigid, authoritarian stance before it's too late. To insist that I—and the thousands for whom I speak—take the consequences of my vocational decision smacks of monolithic totalitarianism and cries out to heaven for redress.

If something isn't done and done quickly, I may be forced—against all my inclinations—to bring my case before the wider forum of the American people. In the few pitiful moments I have managed to snatch for myself in the past year I have been working on a book called *A Modern Layman Looks at His Outdated Marriage*—and it's a lulu, I can tell you that.

Catholic Classics Revisited

Transcendent Baby Talk—
Nellie Organ Superstar

LITTLE NELLIE OF HOLY GOD
by Margaret Gibbons
Newman Press

WIDELY read when it was published in 1949, this deceptively simple biography of "the Violet of the Blessed Sacrament" has tragically fallen into relative obscurity; the publishers have allowed it to go out of print. Until recently there was available an illustrated child's version of Nellie's life (*Little Nellie of Holy God* by Sister Mary Dominic, Bruce, 50¢) but this was a mere popularization of the original and hopelessly inadequate because it fails to record Nellie's utterances in the authentic baby talk in which she delivered them.

Born in Waterford, Ireland, in August 1903, Nellie lost her mother to consumption at a tender age. Her father, an Irish laborer who found it necessary to enlist in the British army, was unable to care for Nellie and her older sister.[1] The girls were sent to the Convent of the Good Shepherd in Cork in the year 1907 when Nellie was three years and nine months old. Both girls were suffering from whooping cough and had to be quarantined until pronounced cured. But Nellie was afflicted with a

[1] Nellie's father's surname was Organ. Miss Gibbons confirms that he was a soldier but does not specify his rank. In the child's version Sister Dominic somewhat unfortunately refers to him as "Private Organ."

crooked spine, as well, the legacy of a careless country girl who had been "looking after" her and let her drop to the floor. However, no one at the convent was aware of this and when Nellie cried and fidgeted about when made to sit upright at her little work desk it was thought that she was simply being horrid. She also bore the fatal spores of T.B. contracted from—as Nellie always called her—"My dead Mommy."

After the nuns discovered the situation they realized that Nellie was a very saintly little girl. She was precocious at her prayers and endlessly thoughtful of others. But author Gibbons is not out to create a plaster saint. She faithfully reveals that Nellie could be naughty on rare occasions as when one evening "through sheer willfulness, she kept six children late for supper, to the great inconvenience of others."

" 'Shame on you!' said the nurse. 'You should make an act of contrition for this.' Nellie was on her knees instantly, addressing herself to Holy God: 'Holy Dod,' she prayed, 'I am berry sorry for teeping de girls late for supper; please forgib me and make me a good child and bless me and my Modders.' "

Instead of overtly telling us of Nellie's very special relationship with God, Miss Gibbons lets it emerge in its tender intensity through direct quotations. Her skill at weaving them into the narrative makes one think of Proust and James and recalls again the great dictum of Ruskin, to let character emerge "like the blooming of a lily, so that only gradually and with mounting excitement do we see the beauty within."[2]

"Modders" was Nellie's name for the sisters, of course, and she loved them dearly. But she would not let her relationship with "Holy Dod" be exploited, even by them. The convent had run up a considerable debt for renovations and one of the sisters, worried about it, came to Nellie's bedside soon after it became apparent that the child hadn't terribly much longer to live. She said to Nellie: "Baby, soon you will be with Holy God; won't you ask Him to send us money so Mother can pay the debts?" The expressive little eyes flashed and without hesitation Nellie answered emphatically: "Him knows and dat's enough."

This is a supremely apt example of what I meant by the inadequacy of a version of Nellie's conversation not rendered in baby talk. How weak and pedestrian if she were made to say: "He is aware and that is sufficient." Miss Gibbons, of course, was meticulous in all aspects of her research. In her foreword, written in 1947, she states: "Nothing that appears in the following pages is set down from hearsay. Every detail has been confirmed to the writer in personal interviews with the nun who was Nellie's Reverend Mother in 1907–1908 (these interviews took place in July, 1928, but I am writing now from their written record) as well as with two other sisters who knew the child intimately."

Thus we can be absolutely sure that the Infant of Prague actually danced for Little Nellie shortly after she made a novena to Him ("one set of devotions for each of the nine months that the Virgin carried

2 Perhaps not Ruskin—quite possibly Studs Terkel.

the Child in her womb"). But let Miss Gibbons describe the incident as told to her by Mary Long, the hired girl who helped the Sisters care for Nellie:

"Mary went into the other room, got the statue and gave it to Nellie. Nellie, now perfectly happy and content, hugged the little image, hushing it in her arms, and kissing it, with many lisping murmurs of affectional apostrophe. Then she put it on the floor beside the pots and pans. . . . Let us now continue in Mary Long's own words: 'Presently Nellie gets very excited and calls out: "Longie, Him dance for me! Longie, play more moosic!" I thought the child had gone mad. Then Josephine, the girl who helped with the cleaning, came in. Josephine at once said, "What is the matter with Nellie?" Nellie, her face flushed, her eyes sparkling, cries out—just flinging one glance toward us, then instantly back again to the statue, "Jo, play moosic: Him dance for me, now me dance for Him," and Nellie begins stepping about, her arms extended. Stopping suddenly, she cries in a disappointed little voice, "Oh, Him 'topped now!" And she is quiet once more.' "

In point of fact, then, the Infant appeared frequently to Nellie, and not only to dance but to personally instruct her in spiritual matters, for Nellie gave evidence of spiritual knowledge far beyond her years. Miss Gibbons bravely confronts those of her readers who might dare to doubt the apparitions:

"Persons who read casually in accounts of St. Rose of Lima of how Jesus seated himself in tiny form on a rosebud in a bowl, to gladden her whilst she worked, have no difficulty at all in accepting the assertion."

Certainly the Sisters knew that Nellie was being given special visions. One in particular who had a similar devotion to the Holy Child, was passing by a statue of the Infant of Prague and "dropped to her knees with a simple prayer, 'Lord, if you really did dance for Little Nellie, please send us a bakehouse.' "

Is it any wonder, then, that in spite of her years, Nellie was eventually allowed to receive Communion and even confirmed by the Bishop! Her powers of spirituality then truly began to manifest themselves in extraordinary ways. As Father Martindale, S.J., said of her: "She was in tune with the holiness of God; she could tolerate the Invisible as if she saw it."

For instance, she could tell when the Blessed Sacrament was exposed in Benediction in the chapel even though she was far away in her room. She could also tell when people had received Communion. When Mary Long failed to go to early Mass one day, Nellie, upon waking several hours later, charged her with not receiving. Dumbfounded, Mary decided to put the child to a test and the next day slammed the kitchen door as if she had left for the chapel. Later she went into her room and greeted Nellie cheerfully but Nellie brushed the greeting aside and "fixing her great eyes on Mary said deprecatingly: 'Longie, you did not get Holy Dod this morning.' "

At the moment of her death Nellie was four years, five months and eight days old. And it is in the recording of this tragic instant that Miss Gibbons soars to the heights of her art. How tempting, with such dramatic material at hand, to overplay, to sentimentalize. But she resists, and more—sublimates the moment:

"All day long the agony was heartrending to behold. Several Sisters came in turn to kneel around the cot. Three remained witnesses of the child's saintly death. Toward three o'clock [notice that Miss Gibbons does not point out the fact that it was at this same hour that Jesus expired on the cross] the little sufferer became quite calm, and she remained motionless for about an hour. Her eyes were fixed on something she seemed to see at the foot of her bed. There was an extraordinary look in those lovely eyes. Then she moved; her eyes now filled with tears. She tried to rise and draw near to that 'Something' on which she gazed so longingly. And then she smiled. From the movement of her lips she seemed to speak with someone, and now raising her eyes, she followed with a look of supernatural love that 'Something' which now seemed to hover above her head. Presently, with an ecstatic smile, Little Nellie's frame relaxed. She had gone to her Holy God forevermore."

To my mind that compares—overshadows—the ending of *A Tale of Two Cities* and puts Victor Hugo to shame. A less scrupulous biographer might have been tempted to interject some heartwarming invention of baby talk like "Dat's all folks," but not Miss Gibbons.

It is with equal restraint that Miss Gibbons describes the extremely touching scene of Nellie's first Holy Communion. For the Bishop could not remain ignorant of her evident sanctity and granted her the dispensation to make her confession and receive Holy Communion in spite of her age. At the time of her death, then, Nellie had received all of the Sacraments except Holy Orders and Matrimony. It is said that Pope Pius X was influenced by Nellie's saga in his monumental decision to let children receive Communion when they attained the age of reason.

Nellie was first interred in the public cemetery but as visitors to her grave began to come in increasing numbers (not a few crutches and braces were discarded and heaped upon it by the grateful cured) the Sisters for some reason began to have second thoughts and had Nellie exhumed and reburied in the Convent graveyard. To the amazement of no one but skeptics the little body was found completely uncorrupted (well, almost) and to this day rests at Sunday Wells in Cork. This magnificent biography is a splendid tribute to a shining life and the fact that it is no longer read by Catholic parents or in Catholic schools is one of the chief reasons why both are in so much trouble.

Our Parish Council Meets

Minutes of the first meeting of the Parish Council of Saint Prometheus Church

Convened at 7:45 p.m. in the newly dedicated Parish Council Assembly Room in the school basement (formerly Brownies and paper drive storage). All officers of the executive committee, members-at-large, designated and honorary members were present with the exception of Mrs. Ronald Birkhoff (Liturgical Committee) whose husband called to say that she had dislocated her hip at a Folk Mass.

DR. CLIVE BARNES, president, called upon Msgr. George McMann (Honorary Member) to give the opening prayer. Mr. Leslie Porash (Christian Unity Committee) asked if it wouldn't be better if the Council said the prayer as a body. Dr. Barnes told Mr. Porash to sit down and shut up. Msgr. McMann said a prayer to the Holy Spirit followed by an ejaculation to the Little Flower. Mr. Porash said he didn't think the Council should pray to the patron of docility. Dr. Barnes told Mr. Porash to shut up again. Msgr. McMann said, no, it was all right, and that members of the Council should feel free to speak their minds. Mr. Porash was probably right, he said, and it would be better if the Council prayed as a body in the future, provided they all knew the words, which he doubted. Dr. Barnes said that Msgr. had prepared a few remarks which he would like to read into the minutes. Mr. Porash said something which the recording secretary (me) missed. Msgr. McMann then read the following statement:

I have carried the load here at St. P's for thirty-three years now, and nobody can say that I've ever dragged my feet about making changes of any kind. I want to go on record as being 100 percent behind this parish council which is called for in the documents of Vatican II. We were the first parish in this part of town to get our altar turned around and while we're not the first parish to get our council on the tracks, we're not the last, by any means. So I'm just here to say that I welcome this opportunity to discuss things with you in an open, constructive way. But at the same time I've got to deal with the real nuts and bolts problems of keeping this big plant of ours humming. You make suggestions and go home, but your priests stay right here on the job twenty-four hours a day. As I said, I'm open to any reasonable suggestions, but I'd be letting you down and I'd be letting the bishop down if I wasted my time trying to implement every half-baked idea that came along. The Vatican Council made it clear that we're all laboring in the same vineyard, but a lot of people have taken that to mean that anybody is free to pick where he pleases. Well, Our Lord had something to say about that a long time before the Vatican Council. You all know the parable about the late-comers getting paid as much as the workers who had borne the heat of the day. Our Lord was upholding the management's right to ultimate authority there in no uncertain terms. Now I don't want you to defer to me just because I'm a priest of God and a Chamberlain to the Holy Father himself, but I do want you to remember that I'm your pastor. Now pastor means shepherd and a good shepherd has got to look out for the best interests of all his sheep. He can't think of only a few of them. That's about it. I want you to think of me as your shepherd and I'm here to tell you that this is one shepherd who's always willing to listen to his sheep.

Msgr. said that this concluded his remarks about policy and if anyone had any questions about it or anything else would they please make it snappy as he had an important appointment with a contractor back at the rectory and would like to see the meeting adjourned by 8:15.

Mrs. Darcy (Education Committee) asked what it was that the Msgr. was going to talk to the contractor about as she wasn't about to authorize any building funds until the school library got a decent budget.

Dr. Barnes told Mrs. Darcy that it wasn't any of her business what the Msgr. talked to the contractor about and that she was only a designated member of the Council so she needn't think she was going to try and run the parish like she tried to run everybody else's business. Mrs. Darcy told Dr. Barnes that he ought to stick to what he knew best which was overcharging people for sloppy fillings and that she had every right to question the Msgr. The parish's money belonged to the People of God, she said, and even if she was just a designated member of the Council, she was still a fullfledged People of God.

Msgr. said that he was afraid that Mrs. Darcy hadn't paid much attention to his opening remarks. Questions like hers were obviously not in the spirit of Vatican II, he said, and she might do well to go home and read the Vatican documents and meditate on their meaning before she popped off to people.

Mrs. Darcy said that if that was the high-handed attitude he was going to take he'd better not look for much in the collection basket from the Darcy family to which Msgr. replied that he was glad she'd warned him or he would never have noticed the difference.

Mrs. Darcy left the meeting.

Dr. Barnes asked if there were any other questions before adjournment.

Mrs. George Petit (Social Life Committee) wondered if the Msgr. had reached any decision regarding the PTA's request that a sheltered bicycle rack be attached to the back wall of the rectory garage to keep the ice and snow off the children's bikes. Her own daughter, she said, had actually frozen to her bike seat just last week and had to be taken inside the house, bike and all, to thaw loose.

Msgr. said yes, he had reached a decision, and it was no. First of all, he said, the rectory garage was heated and this required a special kind of insulated siding which was easily cracked and the kids would undoubtedly ram their bikes into it. Secondly, he was not about to provide a convenient and hidden place right on the playground where the boys could smoke and commit other immoral acts; and thirdly,

if Mrs. Petit would see to it that her daughter was modestly dressed it wouldn't be possible for her to freeze to her bike seat.

Mrs. Petit left the meeting.

Mr. Porash again said something which the secretary missed.

Dr. Barnes then thanked the Msgr. for sparing the Council so much of his time as we all understood that he was a very busy man. The Msgr. said it was his pleasure entirely and that any member of the Council should feel free to approach him at any time between meetings except on Wednesday which was his day off.

Dr. Barnes then asked for a motion to adjourn. Msgr. seconded.

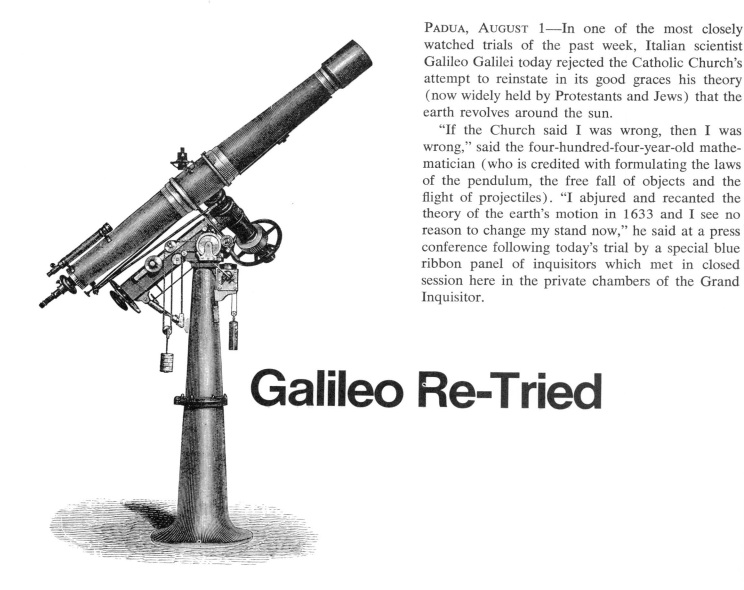

PADUA, AUGUST 1—In one of the most closely watched trials of the past week, Italian scientist Galileo Galilei today rejected the Catholic Church's attempt to reinstate in its good graces his theory (now widely held by Protestants and Jews) that the earth revolves around the sun.

"If the Church said I was wrong, then I was wrong," said the four-hundred-four-year-old mathematician (who is credited with formulating the laws of the pendulum, the free fall of objects and the flight of projectiles). "I abjured and recanted the theory of the earth's motion in 1633 and I see no reason to change my stand now," he said at a press conference following today's trial by a special blue ribbon panel of inquisitors which met in closed session here in the private chambers of the Grand Inquisitor.

Galileo Re-Tried

"That theory was thought up by Copernicus in the first place," the gray-bearded thinker said, "and for a while I thought he was on the right track. Where I went wrong was in teaching it as an established fact when I never had any mathematical proof. And I did so in the face of scripture, tradition and against the Holy Father's express wish that I cease and desist. I don't see what all the fuss is about. People still think of sunrise and sunset—what's the difference which motion causes it."

Said a spokesman for the inquisition: "We are most distressed by Dr. Galileo's stand. It is seldom that the Church gives a man a second chance. We thought he would be delighted at this opportunity to undo the harm he did so wrongfully teaching the truth before the Church had a chance to discover it for itself. But Dr. Galileo has proved to be a most obdurate son of the Church. It's a shame. In the old days we would have had no difficulty making him see things our way."

Xavier Rynne, a correspondent for the *New Yorker* magazine, who claims to have gained access to today's hearing, reports that Galileo denounced the members of the court as "turncoats and underminers of the faith." "He gave them holy hell," said Rynne, who is widely known for his colorful reporting of the Second Vatican Council. "He told them that they were the ones who should be brought to trial for questioning a decision of the Church at a time when papal authority and the Magisterium were already under attack by 'pinkos, free-thinkers, theological perverts and the minions of scientific materialism.' "

According to Rynne, Galileo refused to hear a special plea from Cardinal Koenig or to meet with a delegation of Catholic Nobel Prize-winners who had flown here secretly to honor the scientist at a banquet following the trial.

In Uppsala, news of the trial was received with mixed emotions. Cries of "Three cheers for Galileo!" and "revisionist dog!" swept back and forth across the floor of the assembly and several fist fights were reported. A highly placed spokesman for the World Council of Churches, who requested that he not be identified, said, "I could have told them not to bother—once a Catholic, always a Catholic. If anyone still thinks that ecumenism is more than a paper tiger, this should convince him."

In Rome, observers close to the Vatican told of a brief flurry of unusual activity around the papal chambers and noted that all papal audiences had been cancelled for the balance of the week. An editor of *L'Osservatore Romano,* official organ of the Vatican, declined to comment pending knowledge of what his opinion was going to be.

Meanwhile from Paris, word came that General de Gaulle, who had been following reports of the trial by transistor radio from atop the Sorbonne, had commented: "The truth has been served; the sun, as always, continues to revolve about me."

Second Passing—A Story

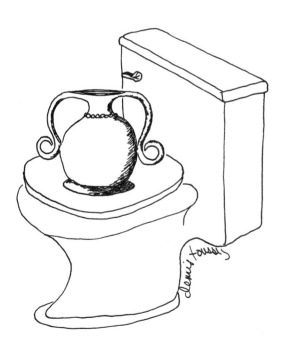

ALL HIS LIFE Herbert had been troubled by a fear of being covered. He was unable to sleep under anything heavier than a single, lightweight blanket and even then suffered frequent nightmares in which he experienced death by suffocation, sometimes by drowning, sometimes by being buried alive.

His will specified that he was to be cremated, his remains "to be placed in an unsealed repository to be kept by my wife among her closest personal effects." Herbert wrote it himself—wills were his specialty—and showed it to Grace on their first wedding anniversary. He reminded her about it at least once a month during the next twenty years.

Accordingly, four days after Herbert's fatal accident, Grace sent his body to Indianapolis for the specified reduction. Hansen Brothers, the local morticians, were not equipped to do the job but agreed to handle the details. The funeral service was held in their chapel, with Herbert lying in a casket from which the lid had been removed (a compromise, Grace realized, which would not have pleased Herbert, but it was either that or a table-top). After the mourners had departed, Herbert, still open-face, was placed in the Hansen hearse and driven the forty-three miles to Indianapolis. Grace and Herbert's twin-but-maiden sister, Florence, followed in Herbert's '55 Chrysler sedan which was appropriately black.

Florence had arrived from Iowa only that morning. She taught English literature in a high school in Cedar Rapids and came to visit Grace and Herbert once each year at Christmas. As Grace feared she might, Florence had arranged for a leave of absence.

"We will walk this road of grief together," she told Grace when she embraced her at the station. From the formidable amount of luggage which followed her off the train, Grace surmised it was going to be a long road.

Back at home late in the afternoon following the funeral, Grace and Florence sat on the sofa in the living room. Florence had placed the urn containing Herbert's ashes on the mantelpiece. After some deliberation she centered it between the Seth Thomas clock and the white Dresden shepherdess which had been her wedding present to Grace and Herbert.

"I want you to know how much I approve your choice of the repository," Florence said, regarding the urn with a benign intensity which softened slightly what was basically the face of a Roman centurian. "You did right to choose something plain and solid—like Herbert." She paused for dramatic effect. " 'Great Beauty with Simple Dignity does not disdain to walk.' "

Grace supposed Florence was quoting from one or another of the minor poets whose excretions she labored so vainly to weld to the tin hearts of her Iowa adolescents. Grace found the urn quite hideous. She had chosen it blindly from the brochure thrust in front of her face by the man at the crematorium. Squat and bulbous, with a mouth almost as wide as its base, it reminded Grace of a miniature cuspidor. She found it difficult to accept as one of her "closest personal effects."

"Herbert was a man of great dignity, you know," Florence said, still declaiming. "He believed in tradition. We were always very much alike, Herbert and I. And close, in the way that only twins are close. We liked the same things. Before he married you we went everywhere and did everything together. We went to the State Fair, to see the plays in Chicago, to the 500-mile race at Indianapolis, to the Kentucky Derby—every year."

"Oh Lord!" Grace said. "I forgot to cancel the hotel reservations in Louisville for this weekend. Herbert and I were going to the Derby."

"Don't cancel the reservations, Grace," Florence said. She jumped up from the sofa and went over to the mantelpiece. "You and I will go to the Derby."

"It's out of the question, Florence," Grace said, genuinely shocked. "Even if I felt like going—which I definitely don't—what would people think of a widow who tore off to a horse race a week after her husband died."

"No one has to know where we're going," said Florence, excitedly. "The change of scene would do you good. And Herbert would want us to go—the Derby was one of his dearest traditions. Our Grandfather Stanford went to the first running of the Derby in 1875, and when our father was old enough, grandfather took him every year—just as father always took Herbert. I doubt if he ever told you, Grace, but it was one of Herbert's bitterest disappointments that he never had any children to take. The least we can do is keep up the tradition for him. Besides," Florence put her hand on the base of the urn, "I see no reason why we can't take Herbert along with us."

Grace did not need Florence to remind her of Herbert's passion for tradition, or about his precious Grandfather Stanford, or about her own childlessness. "Tradition" had killed Herbert. It was his invariable custom to take down the storm windows on the weekend before it was his invariable custom to go to the Derby. Last Saturday he hadn't been feeling well—constipation, he said—but refused to let it throw him off schedule.

"All civilization is based upon the proper observance of ritual," he told Grace in what turned out to be the last words he spoke to her.

Mr. Sommers, the postman, was the only actual eyewitness, though Grace herself heard the crash while she was scouring the tub in the bathroom. Herbert started as usual with the kitchen windows and worked his way up to the second floor north bedroom which faced the street. When Mr. Sommers saw him he was leaning out of the window, lifting the heavy wooden storm sash from its two supporting hooks. As Mr. Sommers described it to the man from the *Weekly Herald* and as the *Herald* (a copy lay on the coffee table in front of Grace) printed it on the front page: "There was Herbert Stanford leaning half-way out the window, balancing the storm sash. Then out he came in the prettiest half-summersault you ever saw, holding the sash in front of him all the way down. The glass flew so far that a piece of it hit my leg. He landed all scrunched up on his head and shoulders and just stayed that way. He never did fall over."

Grace got up and walked into the bay which overlooked the front yard. She parted the curtains and peered out into the twilight. A car was stopped in the middle of the street. Both doors on the driver's side, facing her, were open. A man whom Grace did not recognize was standing in the street pointing up to the second story window above her. Two women sitting in the back seat craned their necks to see. As she watched, the man convoluted his wrist, tracing a summersault in the air. Grace let the curtains fall

back together.

"All right, Florence," Grace said tightly, "let's go to the Derby. We'll leave tomorrow after lunch."

It was close to two o'clock, though, before they got away the next afternoon. Immediately after lunch Florence announced that she had to go downtown to do a little shopping and didn't return until one forty-five. She had purchased a large thermos cork with which to stopper Herbert's urn. Unable to bear the thought of "packing him away like a pair of socks," Florence installed the urn on a cushion in the front seat between herself and Grace and from her position on the right guarded it against the effects of sharp curves and precipitous brakings of the Chrysler. In spite of heavy traffic they arrived at the hotel in Louisville just as the street lights went on.

The Hotel, Grace's principal reason for hating the memory of Grandfather Stanford, was situated close to the river in the oldest part of town. Even since her last visit—three years ago, when she had been unable to come up with a logical reason for not accompanying Herbert on his annual trip—the place appeared to have gone downhill, sharply. The room clerk was an indifferent young man with inordinately long sideburns and the bellboy appeared to have been captured wild and dragged in from the hills only hours ago. All the way up in the elevator (itself a marvel of mechanical antiquity which deserved to hang from the ceiling of the Smithsonian next to Lindbergh's airplane) he viciously masticated a cheek-protruding wad of what Grace could only hope was chewing gum. From the way he unlocked and hurled open the door to their room she was sure he would have much preferred to kick it in. He seized Grace's tip, made a growling noise with the back of his crowded mouth and departed, leaving their bags sitting just inside the door.

"He must be temporary help," Florence said, watching Grace struggle with the suitcases. "When Herbert brought me here they treated us grandly." She opened her ample purse, brought forth the urn, and set it on top of the dresser.

"Hat's off before ladies," Florence said extracting the thermos cork.

Grace was looking at the room's solitary picture: a woodcut showing a Huck Finn type fishing from the end of a crumbling pier. It looked terribly familiar.

"Shall we eat here in the hotel?" Florence asked from behind the closed bathroom door. "Herbert and I always did—the food is delicious." She said something else but her voice, was swept away on a rising tide of noise set loose by her actuation of the hotel's ancient plumbing. A single, startled cry of "Mercy!" was all that Grace could make out above rumblings and gurglings which seemed to spring from the very bowels of the earth.

When the racket subsided, Grace said, "I doubt if the food's as good as it was then, Florence, but I suppose it would be simpler to eat here than to try and drive somewhere in the car."

Looking somewhat pale, Florence emerged from the bathroom. She went to the dresser and began to fix her hair. Grace took another look at the picture. She *had* seen it before: when she and Herbert shared this room three years ago.

"Why don't we call room service," Grace said, "and have a drink sent up before we go down to eat." It would be more seemly than the sight of the two of them swilling away in public and somehow Grace felt very much like having a drink.

"You know that Herbert never approved of drinking in hotel rooms," Florence said. "He always

ordered a Mint Julep for us *after* the Derby."

As she spoke, Florence turned toward Grace in an exact replica of one of Herbert's favorite legal postures: right arm dropping straight down in resignation, the left crooked on an indignant hip. Framed in the triangle of mirror-backed space thus created between Florence's side and arm, the urn glinted its strong seconding disapproval.

Unable to face down the both of them, Grace gave in and went down to the dining room with Florence. An elongated, high-ceilinged specimen of genuine Steamboat Gothic, the room reminded Grace of the Hansen Brothers' mortuary chapel. Florence, however, found the atmosphere exhilarating.

"Isn't this fun, Grace!" she burbled between bites of the breaded veal cutlet dinners they had ordered (Grace, because it was either that or catfish; Florence, because it was Herbert's "favorite restaurant meal"). "If only Herbert were here to enjoy this with us. We should have brought him down—nobody would have noticed our little centerpiece."

Grace found that the thought did little to enhance the taste of her cutlet which, under a soddenly greasy brown crust, was intricately stringed, dead white, and studded with little surprise pockets of phlegm-like fat.

"Have you decided which horse you're going to bet on tomorrow?" Grace asked, hoping to change the subject.

"Herbert always picked my horses for me," Florence said, isolating and severing with surgical relish a vein connecting her last two bites of meat. "He did it by the names—whichever had the most significance for us."

Their waiter, evidently a venerable holdover from the good old days, cleared away the dishes promptly and brought coffee. At Grace's request, and without a grumble, he even provided a newspaper. Grace opened it to the sports page and spread it on the table so that both she and Florence could read the Derby roster.

Grace put her right forefinger on the favorite's name. "What about *Riptide?*" she asked.

"No!" Florence was emphatic. "There's no relation between us and 'riptide.' None whatsoever."

"*Beautiful Ohio,* then?" Grace countered. "We crossed it just this afternoon."

Florence was emphatic again, and slightly shocked. "You know how Herbert hates water."

"Well," Grace said, irritated by Florence's lapse into the present tense, "the only other one I can see with any significance at all is *Merry Widow,* though the Lord only knows I don't feel merry, and it couldn't possibly do for you."

Grace knew that Florence was extremely touchy on the subject of her spinsterhood, but it was too late to apologize, even if she felt like it.

"That was uncalled for, Grace," Florence said, her face puffing into an amazingly swollen pout. "If Herbert were here you wouldn't dare talk to me like that."

"Oh *can* Herbert!" Grace spat back at her. "Herbert is dead. D-E-A-D, dead!"

"I knew it! I knew it all along." Florence delivered the pregnant pout into full fledged, highly audible sobs which reached wetly into the furthest corners of the crowded room. "You've always hated me, haven't you! And I don't think you ever really loved Herbert, either."

Covering her face with her hands, Florence jumped up and ran out of the dining room, across the lobby, and into the waiting elevator.

Conscious of all the eyes on her, Grace deliber-

ately folded the newspaper, paid the waiter, picked up Florence's abandoned purse, and went up to the room. Florence was standing in the corridor outside the door.

"Give me my key, please," she said in a dehydrated voice. "I'm going to have my things moved to another room."

"I very much doubt if there's another room to be had in this town tonight," Grace said evenly, handing Florence her purse. She unlocked the door with her own key and stepped aside to let Florence enter first.

"We'll just see about that," Florence said, moving straight to the phone on the dresser.

Grace sat down on the edge of the bed closest to the door and started taking off her shoes. The beds had been turned back while they were at dinner.

"Well, in that case send someone up for my bags —I'm checking out," Florence told the room clerk imperiously. "And have a cab waiting to take me to the train station."

At the funeral, Grace had observed that when Florence was deeply upset she tended to jerk. Her motions in hanging up the phone reminded Grace of the tragic conclusion of a silent movie, flickering an artificial emotion she found it impossible to share.

"I'm going back to Iowa where I'm appreciated," Florence said in the same regal tones she'd employed on the room clerk. "And, if you don't mind, I'll take Herbert along with me, where he belongs."

Keeping Grace's reflection covered with her eyes, Florence moved her hand intermittently toward the urn. She stopped jerking the instant she picked it up. The difference in weight must have been infinitesimal, but Florence sensed it at once.

"Herbert is gone," she gasped. "Grace, he's gone!"

Moving quickly from the bed Grace passed behind Florence and snatched the urn from her up-raised hand in a fair rendition of the old Statue of Liberty play. She held the urn over the glass top of the dresser and tilted it gradually over until it stood completely upside down.

"The maid," Grace said.

Florence stood transfixed, her hand still upraised. She moved her jaws rapidly up and down, but aside from a dry, clicking noise, verbalized nothing.

"She must have thought it was an ashtray," Grace said. "Help me check the wastebasket." Grace felt amazingly detached and scientific.

It was as if her words plugged Florence into a wall socket. She tore into the bathroom with Grace padding along in stocking-footed pursuit. But the interior of the plastic container they found behind the door gleamed with an almost virginal whiteness. The toilet, however, was another matter. The water in its massive, ancient bowl bore strong traces of a dark, powdery flotation.

"Herbert!" Florence screamed, dropping to both knees with an abandon that would have done credit to an acrobat. "Don't worry, Dear, we will save you."

She looked wildly up at Grace. "The urn, Grace. Get the urn so we can scoop him up."

Grace started back to the dresser where Herbert's deserted shell still stood inverted upon the glass. "He never did fall over," she couldn't help remembering.

There was a savage knock at the corridor door. "Bellboy," said an extremely surly voice.

Florence's open suitcase shouted silent threats of forgiveness and reconciliation from the luggage stand. Heeding it like a clarion call, Grace spun around and went noiselessly back into the bathroom. Reaching over the still kneeling Florence who now embraced the cold porcelain oval, Grace leaned forward from the waist, stretched forth her arm, and flushed the toilet.

No More Chicken Soup for You, Philip Roth

**or Mrs. Portnoy's Complaint
or My Son, The Schlemiel**

Dear Alex:

We've read the book, your father and me, and you'll understand, I'm sure, why you should drop dead. Compared to you, Benedict Arnold was a regular Moshe Dayan, though I shouldn't libel poor Ben by mentioning your name in the same breath—he was probably good to his parents.

Swing low, sweet Iscariot! If I could get my hands on you and your cute "as-told-to" friend, Phil Roth, you'd both be blowing soap bubbles under your olives at the fancy Uptown parties the big shots at Random House will be throwing for you between sessions of selling your mother and father. Such lies I haven't heard since your bar mitzvah!

Such filth I haven't seen since I was forced to use the "ladies" in the Newark bus station!

What an imagination! Sick as it is, I have to hand it to you. You could get sex from a pair of bagels— or even one! I come with the bread knife to the table and I'm castrating you, yet. I look for cinders in your ear and I'm violating your inner sanctum with a Q-Tip. Mrs. Freud, even, didn't have such a son!

So I asked your father—whom all the world now knows as "the constipated wonder"—"Where did we go wrong?" And do you know what he said, this broken man who can never go out of the house again without somebody offering him a milk of magnesia tablet: "It must have been the way we went about having him—he didn't approve of our method."

Everybody is giving me quotes from your book, so you won't mind if I ask you (when you can free a hand!) to take a look at the bottom of page 247: "A nice little Jewish boy? Please, I am the nicest little Jewish boy who ever lived! Only look at the

fantasies, how sweet and savior-like they are! Gratitude to my parents, loyalty to my tribe, devotion to
the cause of justice!" You'll pardon me while I
choke. To recommend it, however, it's the only
clean paragraph for pages. And I'm not talking
Irving Wallace, I'm talking Gore Vidal! When Mrs.
Voxman, the postman's wife who's so big with her
book clubs, tells me about *Myra Breckenridge,* I'm
thinking: "Who could possibly write filthier than
that." It does a mother's heart good to get the answer on the front page of the newspaper—your own
little boy, your pure and shining star!

I hear they're making a movie of it. Do yourself a
favor, please, and tell them to wait till your father
and I are dead—which won't be long now, thanks
to you. Otherwise you won't be able to help out
much with the script—at five big ones a week, as
they say in *M. B.*—except by long-distance from the
jail we'll put you in from suing like nobody's been
sued since Errol Flynn. What kind of movie can you
make inside a bathroom, anyway, Cool-Hand Alex?
Maybe you think there are thousands of Jewish boys
who are going to thank you for socking it to mama,
huh? Listen, there's not a teen-ager between here
and Tel Aviv who's going to get by with locking the
bathroom door for the next fifty years. A new commandment there's going to be—"Thou shalt not
Portnoy."

O.K., Mr. Wise-Guy, that's all I have to say. This
is where I used to tell you to be sure to wear your
rubbers when it's raining. I couldn't care less if you
ran barefoot through the Suez Canal, so why don't
you.

Your mother, the Victim

I GUESS some of you have been wondering when I would get around to talking about the new encyclical on birth control. Well, actually, it's not *just* about birth control. It's called *Humanae Vitae*—"Of Human Life"—and that's a big subject, a very big subject indeed. We could talk about the positive aspects of human life for a long time and not even begin to make a dent in the subject. The Pope stresses the dignity of life and the need to protect it from the insidious encroachments of materialism and hedonism and things like that. And the sanctity of marriage. There are lots of forces militating against that, you can be sure. . . .

Now the Bishop has asked that we all read this encyclical and form our consciences accordingly. You all heard Monsignor Doughty read the Bishop's letter last week. Well the Bishop also sent word that there was to be a sermon preached on the subject today in every parish and I guess this is it. It's a shame that Monsignor Doughty couldn't give it himself, being the pastor and all. But as you all . . . well, I mean . . . he's under the weather again.

Some of you have called to say that you weren't altogether happy with the encyclical or with the Bishop's letter. But then some others called to say

Father Custer Takes a Stand

that it was about time and where did I think it left me after all my talk. . . . It seems I've taken on a sort of liberal image around here which isn't altogether justified in spite of some of the things I've preached about in the past . . . family limitation and celibacy. But I don't think I was ever really *for* birth control. I believed in what the Council called "responsible parenthood" and that in some circumstances this might work itself down to limiting—for serious reasons, of course, that's always understood—to limiting the number of children in a family. And then, of course, some people claim that rhythm didn't work very well for them and asked me if it wouldn't be all right if they took the pill for a while.

Well, as you may recall, there was a lot of talk about freedom of conscience then—right after the Council, I mean—and I may have gotten a little carried away and told a few people that it *seemed* to me that it *might* be a matter for them to decide individually, with the advice of their doctor, of course. But I want to make it perfectly clear that I never went around telling people that they should use the pill. You've got to remember that there was —there seemed to be—some question of doubt then. The theologians talked a lot about that; practically every magazine and paper carried articles to that effect—that there was doubt and while there was doubt people were free to follow their own consciences. Why, some of those same theologians still seem to think that there's considerable room . . . some leeway . . . but. . . .

The thing is that the Pope has spoken now and the Bishop has spoken and Monsignor Doughty has spoken and . . . well, then there's the natural law as plain as the nose on your face and tradition besides that. It's not infallible, though. Even Rome admits . . . I mean, very few things we believe as Catholics have actually been pronounced *ex cathedra,* 100 percent infallible. But we believe them just the same, don't we? It would certainly take somebody with a great deal of pride to set themselves up as knowing more than the Pope, the Holy Father, especially in matters of faith and morals. You'd have to be awfully sure of yourself to do a thing like that. Not many people would dream of doing such a thing . . . well there was Martin Luther—people like that.

And you can be sure that the Holy Father didn't just sit down and dash this encyclical off. No. He agonized over the question for years and if you'll go to the trouble to read *Humanae Vitae* for yourselves and not go by what *Time* magazine and some of these progressive . . . radical . . . Catholic papers tell you you should be thinking about it—if you do that, you'll be able to see that the Holy Father went into every conceivable . . . I mean imaginable . . . aspect of it. He wasn't writing it just to spoil everybody's fun . . . I mean the joys of exercising your conjugal rights. Which is what some of these secular and radical papers would have you believe.

No. It would have been a lot easier for the Pope . . . the Holy Father to give in to all this popular pressure. But it's not his job to win popularity contests. He looked at all the facts and prayed over them and made his decision. He shut himself off from the world . . . well, not in that sense exactly. He felt it was too big . . . too complex . . . too delicate a problem to be dealt with effectively by the Vatican Council. There were hundreds of bishops there, speaking all sorts of languages and it would have taken them forever to arrive at a consensus. Then he set up a special commission composed of experts—doctors, theologians, Cardinals, even lay people—to study the question and give him their *opinion*. Even they couldn't reach a unanimous decision, some of them anyway . . . I mean a majority is not unanimity, not by a long shot. So it was left to the Holy Father to decide and he did.

Well, that's about all. I guess it's pretty clear where I stand. I know that most of you will take this in your stride. It's never been easy to be a Catholic. Nobody ever told us it would be easy, did they? But if there are still some who find it hard to accept . . . nobody expects you to take this lying down . . . er . . . but don't do anything rash. It can all be worked out with your confessor. Nobody's going to consign you to the fire and brimstone. Come to me and we'll talk it over in private. It would be better if you came to me, I mean. Monsignor Doughty doesn't hear many confessions these days anyway because what with the overcrowding of the school and all he doesn't have much time . . . anyway it would be best if you saw me. I mean I didn't expect this any more than . . . there's a faint possibility that . . . of . . . but it really . . . oh, well. . . . Amen.

Death of a Dog

ITEM: *A dog was struck and killed by a car at 9:30 last night on the highway north of town, an unidentified boy reported to the police this morning.*

Put Out More Dogs

after Evelyn Waugh

"MYLES! I DO WISH you could remember to steer to the right."

Lady Distraught dug bone-white fingers even deeper into the leopard-skin upholstery of the Rolls and glared at her husband.

"Damned nuisance!" His Lordship muttered, veering the wheel sharply to avoid a large moving-van already half off the road and heading for the safety of a concrete embankment.

Trust the Americans to muck up a perfectly simple thing like motoring. During the war, he remembered, some Lend-Lease-happy idiot had come before Parliament with a proposal to make England "keep to the right to make the Yanks feel at home." The fool had gone on to read a forty-minute tract about "not having to change the roads, you know, not even the centerstripes."

Well, he'd dodged more than his share of Americans at home, let them dodge him over here. And, having retrieved the hand with which he had been adjusting his tails to a better lie (they had a terrible propensity to bunch against leopard-skin), he steadied the Rolls for a fresh charge.

A promising petrol tanker was just settling into his sights when Lady Distraught gave one of her well-known screams and something struck the car's right fender with a thud.

"Clement Attlee!" swore His Lordship, sure that he had run up against one of those rural American types whose clothing is covered over with copper rivets and buttons, "that's bound to have marred the finish."

The Weakling and the Dog

after François Mauriac

IT WAS during the summer of his fourteenth year that the dog had been destroyed. His parents, in the manner of those who have only sons who are frail, ran continually to bearded physicians who assured them that all that was required was a month under the sun at X, on the coast. Heeding this divine word as faithfully as had the Israelites in going out of Egypt, they fled the city, driving their firstborn and animals before them, until they came to a halt beside the sea.

But the waters had neither divided nor performed to prescription and the boy had grown thinner while a certain cough, muted in the din of Paris, became more audible in nights as silent as a tabernacle. They baked and watered him by day and rubbed and wrapped him at night until his body became as pliable and porous as a pudding. The days ached on interminably to the drone of his mother's reading and the snuffling sounds which rose from behind his father's newspaper.

The dog had been his great consolation. On the beach it leaped and circled his chair, attacking the waves impetuously with a bravado both comic and inspiring. At night, after the droning and the snuffling in the adjoining room had merged themselves in a rich counterpoint of snoring, the dog would leap over the sill of the boy's room and settle himself in the blankets over his feet.

But doctors, as everyone knows, are able to see far more than ordinary men, and it was not long before one of them discovered dog hairs among the boy's bedclothes.

"And you ask why he coughs and grows thinner," pronounced Zeus from the hallway outside his room.

"But he is so attached to the beast that he will never consent to being separated," his mother responded in the voice of one who knows that what they are saying is of no consequence.

"Here is what you must do. . . ." The doctor outlined his murderous plot without the least diminution of his superbly professional voice.

The Old Dog and the Cars

after Ernest Hemingway

HE WAS AN OLD DOG and he had not chased a car for four years. But he would chase a car tonight and the boy would see him and know that he was not afraid.

He had not been afraid when he was a pup. There were not enough cars on the highway then, or big enough, or fast enough. He took them as they came, every afternoon with the sun in their eyes so they could not see him, which tripled the risk. Or at night, when there was no moon, he had run with risk so big he could feel it crowding against his flank.

There was a Sunday in his third year when he ran four Buicks within ten minutes, making three of them cross the centerline and putting the last one in the ditch. The boy had given him a tire for that.

But the Ford got him the very next day, driven by a woman. She hooked to the right, catching him on the rusty bumper so that he had lost his footing and fallen before the feet of the boy. And the fear had moved up from the tip of his tail and strangled his courage as he lay there.

He did not run again and the boy got another pup. For four years he sat in the afternoon dust under the porch and listened to the applause of brakes on the highway. Tonight they would squeal for him.

The Matter of a Hound

after Graham Greene

THE OVERHEAD FAN moved no faster than the minute hand of his watch. A fly clung to the underside of the blade with contemptuous ease. Through the open door the heat bulged in at him like a penny balloon filled with water. At any moment it would burst and inundate him in his own sweat. Under the porch lizards stirred and rubbed against each other with the sound of dry sticks.

Inspector Hoad opened the bottom drawer of his desk and took out a bottle. Frowning, he held it before his mouth but did not drink.

"Drunk again!" buzzed the fly, "drunk before eight in the morning."

He opened his lips and let the gin slide over his tongue and down the desolate road of his throat. Very quickly, Hoad hoped, it would reach his soul.

The balloon burst. Sweat oozed over his lashes into his eyes and the station-yard began to shimmer through the doorway like the high-noon prospect of an English country pond. Something white was moving across its surface. Slender and white: a swan? The swan stopped in the doorway surrounded by a salty nimbus.

"You killed him," the boy said. "You were drunk and you ran over him but you didn't have to stop because you are the police."

Hoad blotted his eyes on the encrusted khaki sleeve of authority. So it had come to that at last: one night you finally succeed in capturing that elusive nymph, oblivion, and in the morning a boy in a white shirt comes and stands in your door to tell you that you've killed someone.

"You have the only car," the boy said, passing sentence.

Reverently, Hoad recapped the gin and placed it back in the drawer. The moment was too sacred to spoil with sordid curiosity. This boy, Manuel, would tell it well in his careful mission-school English: "He looked at me but did not ask whom it was that he had killed."

To Hoad's lips the barrel of the pistol felt even cooler than had the bottle.

Juventutem Meam

THE thing is, of course, that Catholic kids today have got it hopelessly soft. To begin with, they don't have to go to Mass every day like we did—eight years at eight o'clock, girls in front, boys in back where Sister could keep an eye on them. Somewhere along about the sixth grade, the grip of the Depression relented and we got padded kneelers and I'm here to tell you that I haven't gloried in any physical sensation, including sex, half as much as the first time I settled my ravaged knees into that plastic-covered rubber. Before that you just hung in there, shifting knees and pulling up until your knuckles turned white. I wasn't heavy enough (in those days) to be much good at the sport of elbow-tension, which was how we killed the longest stretch of kneeling time between the Sanctus and the Agnus Dei. What you did was to get the boy at each end of the pew to lock his hands and brace one elbow against the corner post. Then the next guy in locked his hands and braced his elbows against those of the guys on each side of him so that you got this terrific pressure building up without it looking like anything was going on. Then, if you did it right, the weakest link in the chain would shoot straight up in the air about two feet. It was generally me and it was generally right before the elevation. ("Bless me Father, I committed adultery with others, of the same sex, in Church, during Mass.")

If you went to communion you got to eat breakfast in the classroom while the nonreceivers (generally the fruit of mixed marriages) had to start working a bunch of arithmetic problems. Also, you got a gold star on your chart, too, but that was nothing compared to eating a chocolate covered donut while others looked for impossible common denominators. We had a very pious class.

Certain guys who, in later life, turn out to be very successful corporation executives are born to be Traffic Guards. They are let out of class early to assume their posts and get to wear white chest straps and silver badges and are generally pukes. Others, like me, are made into Mass servers, and are usually nice guys who don't ever amount to much. They turned you into servers early in those days on the theory that younger boys were purer. By the time you hit puberty you were washed up and burnt out. So, before I learned the multiplication tables I was taught to rattle off the Latin responses to the Mass, which, like riding a bike, you never forget, no matter how hard you try. My wife tells me I still mumble Latin in my sleep occasionally, when I'm exhausted or have been particularly nasty to the kids.

In addition to the parish church, our school supplied servers for the Little Sisters of the Poor Home for the Aged and to the Poor Clare Cloistered Convent. We worked on three-week shifts, rotating through the three places with a week off between shifts. I've married and buried the population equivalent of a good-sized town and lit enough candles to make Father Keller and his Christophers cry quits. The softest touch was the parish church, because it was reasonably warm in the winter and the earliest Mass was at 6:30. The Little Sisters of the Poor, on the other hand, were just that, and they kept their old people healthy by sparing them the dehydrating effects of central heating. Everything was scrubbed to the nub but everything nonetheless smelled very badly. You had to change from your street shoes to sneakers so you wouldn't scratch the sanctuary floor. And the old folks inevitably found your shoes and removed the laces, no matter where you hid them or how hard you knotted them together.

But the real adventure was the Poor Clare Convent. Their Mass was at six which meant a five o'clock reveille and a long bike-ride across half the town. The convent, or monastery as it was called, occupied a good part of a city block and was completely enclosed by a ten-foot brick wall. When the Ku Klux Klan made its latter-day revival in the Midwest there had been some nastiness aimed at the Poor Clares for being strange, secretive and Catholic. After a cross was burned in front of the convent gate, the Knights of Columbus turned out the next day and topped off the wall with jagged pieces of beer bottles (which the Knights somehow knew where to find) set in mortar. That had been twenty-five years earlier but the wall and the broken glass still stood as a reminder that ecumenism had still to overcome.

To wheel up on a pitch-black winter morning, open the iron gates and commit yourself to the inner fastness was roughly equivalent to solo trick-or-treating at Dracula's castle. Inside a little arched doorway was a small room where your cassock and surplice had been laid out by invisible hands. The little room opened into the sanctuary which was itself nothing but a larger room with no church in front of it. Instead there were two massive grilles covered by long velvet drapes. The Poor Clares were back there chanting away in what must have been beautiful form, but which scared what little hell there was left out of me.

After I suited up I went out and rang a brass bell and lit the candles. Then old Father Louis, who always appeared from his own little room on the other side of the sanctuary, would come out and say Mass. The curtains never opened but I was conscious

of ranked tiers of Sisters with their eyes peeled for the least fidget or twitch. Father Louis had come from the Old Country a long time ago but English was always going to sit uncomfortably on his German tongue. His big and enduring concern was the Marxist conspiracy. He preached on this to the cloistered nuns, warning them over and over against the dangers of becoming infected by atheistic Communism. Communists were everywhere at work undermining the bulwark of Mother Church. Eternal vigilance was the only cure. I got so I saw Communists behind every telephone pole and mailbox. The place was crawling with them, all trying to get at the sisters.

I worried about them but I wasn't above trying to sneak glimpses of their faces when they received communion through a little gold door in the wall. Father Louis generally blocked my view, but I saw a nose once or twice, and part of a mouth. ("Bless me Father, I looked at consecrated virgins.") There was a kindly extern Sister but she obviously wasn't happy about being out front and materialized only infrequently. At Christmas and Easter a handsome basket of candy was set out by my cassock.

Then one night my mother got a call. One of the Poor Clare's had died and I had been selected to assist at the funeral, along with two other long-time servers. We convened next morning and, after the Funeral Mass, Sister Extern handed me the processional cross. But where would we process to? Only then it dawned on me that we were going to be admitted to the inner sanctum.

In the sanctuary the drapes were suddenly pulled apart and the great grille swung open. Like a missionary Alice going through the glass I held the six-foot cross in front of me and stepped into the unknown. There were nuns, fewer than I'd imag-

ined, but lined up in rows with partial black veils covering pale faces. The first huge and almost empty room opened into a long corridor which we traversed Indian-file behind a guiding Sister who never recognized our presence by so much as a nod. Right angle down another corridor, up some steps and down more until I was hopelessly turned around. Finally we went through a narrow archway and down stone steps that wound around and around. They ended in a large crypt. At the far end the dead nun was laid out flat on the floor resting on a large board. A plain wooden coffin sat against the wall directly under the deep hole which had been opened to receive it. A large bucket of steaming wet mortar with a trowel stuck in it rounded out the gala setting.

The dead nun had no veil on, and there was just enough space between her head and the end of the room for me to plant myself and the cross. Father Louis and my colleagues took up their stand at her feet. Father Louis began his prayers, punctuating them with with heavy splats of holy water which criss-crossed the dead nun's habit like machinegun bullets. I had never seen a dead person at such close quarters, and the finality of "deadness" came home to me emphatically as I watched the holy water roll down that stony forehead and into the corner of an unblinking eye.

There was not a tear to be seen in any other eye, however, nor any sobs to be heard. The only sound was Father Louis droning on and on in his guttural Latin. When he was done, two elderly caretakers shuffled in, picked up the board, nun and all, put it into the coffin, nailed the lid shut, slid it into the wall and, while we trooped back up the winding steps, began to splash on the mortar. Nobody could accuse those nuns of getting sentimental about death—I'd seen puppies buried with more loving care. I didn't understand, of course, but it remains one of the most cold-blooded sights I've ever witnessed.

It wasn't long afterwards that puberty began to manifest its awful effects upon my voice and thus revealed to be on the verge of concupiscence, I was cashiered from the ranks of servers forever.

And not a day too soon.

I Remember Papa

TWO days in bed with a sneaky virus and a copy of the Hemingway novel *Islands in the Stream* and I began to think the thermometer was a fishing rod. There were times when I must have been delirious because one stretch of eighteen pages seemed to have the hero, an internationally famous painter named Thomas Hudson, talking to and about his pet cats. Fish, cats, lots of drinks, a goldhearted prostitute, bars, boats, fights and a rousing but fatal chase after the crew of a sunken U-boat all mixed up with those tiny timepills exploding in my stomach. I didn't catch a thing trolling off the end of the bed.

No doubt the critics will be after this one like sharks. It goes to 466 pages and can't fight back—posthumous Papa resurrected by Miss Mary and Charles Scribner, Jr., for $10 and the Book-of-the-Month-Club. I can't help it. I liked it. It killed the virus.

In *Notes from a Sea Diary,* a book designed to scuttle all the land-bound critics who helped drive Hemingway to bay in front of his own shotgun, Nelson Algren says that he met Ernest only once, and briefly. But he remembers distinctly that Hemingway gave him a portentous message: "It is now 2030 hours." Algren got that during a Christmas visit at the *finca* outside Havana and still liked Hemingway. But hell, I knew Hemingway a lot less well than that and I liked him too.

* * *

"There lies Heeemingway boat," the Havana cop with a submachine gun on his lap told me as we were going sixty along the waterfront.

"The Pilar?" I responded knowledgeably, opening my eyes in a brave but tardy effort to identify the spot. I told myself that I'd come back and hang around in the hope that Hemingway would arrive with Ava Gardner and Ingrid Bergman and offer to take me fishing with him. He was supposed to have a soft spot for servicemen. There was always the chance. But what if he took me and I didn't fish bravely and well and truly disgraced myself? At the moment it was enough to have ridden by the Pilar in a police car, scattering pedestrians like mullet in our wake. It turned out to be a very Hemingway sort of day for me. If I'd had his complete works in compact form I would have eaten them for courage. Batista's Havana in 1954 was a good place to separate editors and critics from real writers.

Shore Patrol Officer for twenty-four hours in one of the off-limits precincts around Las Animas Hospital—a token gesture, an Ensign and Chief Petty Officer to count the bodies and save the embassy a sticky phone call at 3 A.M. Some enterprising researcher in the ship's office made the discovery that I'd had two years of college Spanish and would be just the man to unsnarl the legal difficulties resulting from locking up half the sailors from three visiting American ships. Had they bothered to consult me they would have learned that my two-years of Spanish wasn't good enough to obtain basic necessities, much less preserve international relations. Working up a bad tourist blister the day before, I had tried to purchase a band-aid from two shops and a corner stall. In each instance I had dramatically pointed to my foot and asked for "un bandito." What I got were two contraceptives and a bag of potato chips. I tried to explain that being Catholic I couldn't use the rubber goods and that the chips were too salty, but the proprietors only shrugged and walked away.

The cops ran us around the district by way of reconnaissance for the evening patrol. Thirty-seven bars and fourteen houses but everything, at this afternoon hour, calm and peaceful—not an American sailor in sight. I cheered up. Off limits must mean off limits. But the Chief Petty Officer, a hard-bitten man, kept right on making notes of the addresses of all the houses.

We arrived at precinct headquarters about five. It was a marvelous building in pink marble, just a shade less grand than the Taj Mahal. They showed me to an empty desk. I put my whistle and clipboard on it and sat down. Law and order was going to be a snap. The Chief disappeared.

I watched the night shift come in. Playful fellows, one and all, they horsed around with loaded Thompsons. A little muzzle-feint here, a little barrel-jab there. Then they stood the guns up in a row against the marble wall about thirty feet from me. (It was o.k., though, because the butts rested on the equally slick marble floor.) I looked for things under my desk. That was the first of many mistakes I would make. There was a none-too-ancient human skull down there with a big hole in it where none should have been; a sandwich wrapped in brown paper was stuck between the jaws. I was glad I didn't find a whistle around its no-neck but decided I'd forego the sandwich.

Everybody stopped horsing around when the Commandante, a truly elegant man in a uniform that would make Nixon drool, came out to look over the shift. It was Friday night and he was clearly on his way back to the fort but, spotting me behind my

desk (no mean trick in itself), he graciously invited me into his office. Nixon would have coveted that, too. It was so big it had a horizon. Over the fire place was an oil of Batista wearing a uniform only slightly grander than the Commandante's. The one stripe on my rumpled coat shriveled up and died.

El Cid offered me a cigar which I took, but no brandy from the cutglass decanter on his desk, which I would have taken too. Basil Rathbone couldn't have come across the language barrier better. "An unpleasant duty, but a necessary one that we both perform," he told me. He made it crystal clear that the part of Havana I would be scanning was not his neighborhood. He had a boy in a Catholic military school in Georgia, a sailing yacht and a hacienda in the suburbs. He concluded by indicating, with great tact, that the best thing I could do would be not to interfere, leave everything to his men and simply stay out of the way. It sounded like great advice so I thanked him and went out to look for the Chief.

It took me three hours to find him. He was having a beer in the parlor of the busiest house in the district. I found it by following the steady stream of sailors moving in and out the door. These rascals were all out of bounds but didn't seem a bit disturbed by the big SP armband I was wearing. But who would catch the end of the stick when the word got back to headquarters? Me, that was who.

I got in line and worked my way upstairs where I discovered the Chief. He'd made a lot of friends in a short time it seemed, and he assured them that I was not the sort to make trouble. The madame smiled at me and with a sweep of her bangled arm indicated that I should take my pick of the girls in the room, "on the house"—an etymological irony which escaped me at the moment. I yelled at the

Chief to get the hell back to the station and fled into the night.

Back at my desk I called Shore Patrol Headquarters and told them that the whole fleet was out of bounds to the man. How many of them should I arrest? Could I please have some help, as the Chief wasn't working out too well? The man on the other end of the line yawned and asked if there was a brawl in any of the houses? Was there riot and bloodshed on the streets? Was anybody complaining about being overcharged? Hadn't they offered me freebies? No? Then what the hell was I bothering headquarters about? He hung up.

I still had visions of a court martial with me as the star. Finally, I remembered what the Commandante had told me about leaving everything to his men. A word to the duty officer and all would be well. But the Commandante's men were all occupied back in the cellblock. They had "arrested" a half-dozen prostitutes, put them into individual cells, and were collecting money from a line of male "visitors" queued up outside the back door. No wonder the Commandante could afford the tuition at a Catholic school.

I went back to my desk and sat down. What would Hemingway do in such a situation, I asked myself. I got no answer so I decided to consult with my friend underneath the desk. The sandwich was gone from his mouth, but he still wasn't talking. It was way past 2030 hours so I decided to join him and went to sleep with my whistle and clipboard close at hand, ready for instant action against the forces of corruption everywhere.

* * *

I never did go back and stand waiting by the Pilar. Somebody told me later that Hemingway was out of the country then, anyway. I did take one of the ship's boats to troll for marlin in the Gulf Stream out beyond the Morro. They were there in abundance, great curved fins darting on all sides of us. And sure enough, I missed them all, bravely and truly and well.

Consumer's League Report on Pastors for Laymen and Curates

Since it was obviously impossible to test every one of the nation's 17,670 resident pastors (Official Catholic Directory), CL's researchers came up with four statistically typical types and purchased 1974 models of each. As you know, CL strives for absolute impartiality and will not make any recommendations contrary to public interest. In this case we feel obliged to report that a serious SAFETY HAZARD exists in all models tested: In situations of extreme operational stress they tend to blow up and spout dangerous rhetoric in all directions. *Until this deadly defect is remedied we cannot recommend unqualifiedly* any *model for prolonged parish use. Readers are therefore put on notice that they will be handling a HIGH RISK product no matter what choice they make.*

(Note: Unless otherwise indicated all models are celibate.)

Model 1

OLDER URBAN IRISH CURMUDGEON

The "Model T" of pastors, many are still in service years after newer and flashier models have come and gone. Features rugged design, few moving parts (except the mouth) which are interchangeable and easily serviced. High resistance to change and liturgical innovation though some come equipped with exterior modifications which make them appear to be of post-Vatican II design. Good mileage obtained on a mixture of corned beef, potatoes and whiskey. The homiletic range is very limited with a strong tendency for the wheels to lock and go in circles. Tremendous power in building drives and excellent collection-counting speed. Recharging of batteries is best accomplished in warm conditions, such as prevail in Florida.

General Remarks: Good for the long haul on straight, bumpy road. Worst defect: Boils over at any mention of sex or contraception.

Model 2

ALL-PURPOSE RURAL DEMAGOGUE

Extremely powerful speaker coupled with sensitive ears, sharp eyes and a transistorized gossip-tuner make this model hard to ignore. Equipped with "instant on" starting, there is, oddly enough, no apparent way to shut it off. Colorful but blurry homiletic images suggest that the chassis generates considerable static and distortion. Multiple antennae plug into business, home and political facilities for around-the-clock surveillance of manners and morals. Heavy resistors counteract all ecumenical interference.

General Remarks: Due to high operating temperatures, needs frequent service and requires second and sometimes third collections to keep it functioning. However, once properly installed it is virtually indestructible and impossible to replace.

Model 3

EX-CHANCERY OFFICE SUPERSTAR

The consumer who gets this model should be aware that it is generally in consequence of the bishop's decision to dispose of fairly well-used merchandise that he is fond of and wishes to reward. Model 3 is essentially a gourmet item, far too expensive and highly seasoned for ordinary family consumption. Despite a handsome and well-packaged look, excellent color and smooth taste, our researchers found an unacceptably high fat and chicken content. Curates will find themselves not only expected to do all the parish work but to digest countless stories of the good old days as well.

General Remarks: This model tends to stay out late and avoid the box and the school with equal facility. Will be abnormally developed in one area with consequent weaknesses in others. Strong predilection for solving problems on paper but bruises easily in actual contact. Comes complete with Carte Blanche and American Express cards, and season ticket to Notre Dame games.

Model 4

MYSTICUS INTERRUPTUS

Of all those tested, this model can be least recommended since it was made to perform in a different environment—the hereafter. Thus its function is largely decorative and inspirational, but not without value in instilling piety and virtue in parishioners hardy enough to rise for the 5:00 A.M. mass which Model 4 prefers to celebrate on Sunday. Otherwise tends to stay alone in his room, regarding any intrusion of the mundane as time stolen directly from God. Curates may prefer this arrangement at first, since they can do pretty much what they please. However, research indicates that parishioners are quick to blame them for anything that goes wrong while attributing all worthy accomplishments to the holiness of the pastor. Model 4 offers considerable savings in that it consumes very little food and prefers to spend vacations on retreat at Trappist monasteries.

General Remarks: Frowns on all parish parties, bazaars, radio, television, movies, pre- and post-marital sex, and will not converse with women in groups under 100. Keeps key to car hanging behind crucifix in his room and considers all excursions from the rectory after 8:00 P.M. (except for sick calls—and somebody had better be dead the next day) as direct occasions of mortal sin. Will not accept ads for parish bulletin; gives mass stipends to the missions; will permit only *Our Sunday Visitor* and *The Register* inside the rectory. Curates who operate under Model 4 are automatically exempt from purgatory.

Six Versions of a Prayer You've Heard

HIPPIE OR
MALCOLM BOYD VERSION

Hey Dad!
You're really out there,
Your name's a blast,
Make our scene as cool as yours.
Spread
A little bread around our pads,
But don't zap us, like,
We don't burn straights when they bug us.
From work in all its forms,
Please steer us clear.
And keep Ronald Reagan off our backs.
How 'bout it, man?

TRADITIONALIST VERSION

Right Reverend God,
Who resides in that big chancery in the sky,
Live up to your Old Testament reputation
And get things back in order here below.
Give baptized, practicing Catholics
Their rights and privileges,
And forgive us for Vatican II,
Just as we will try to forgive
Those sneaky Jews.
Lead us not into experimental liturgies
But deliver us from the Dutch Cathechism.
Amen.

84

Somewhere

EMERGED LAYMAN'S VERSION

Dear Chairman of the People of:
May your name head all petitions,
Your discussion club thrive,
Your pastor admit,
He's out of it.
Give us equal voice to say
Who shall come and who will stay,
As that triumphant bishop whom
We can forget but not forgive
For leading us into building drives.
But deliver us from lay teachers.
Bye.
(*Enclosed find 6 tickets for the CFM Dance*).

NEW BREED PRIEST'S VERSION

Celibate Father, here's your chance
To join our union here below
And show
The Ordinary how you bleed
For our *so* pressing need.
Give us salaries, cars and things,
But no rigid laws or structures,
Please nota.
Yet keep us fairly close to mom,
And spare us from the mission quota.
O.K.?

ADMINISTRATIVE
OR L. B. J. VERSION

My fellow American
In Neutral Outer Space,
May you get a better press than me.
Your Great Society spend and spend,
Your term in office never end.
Balance our budget if you can,
And forgive us our cookouts
As we forgive Bobby Baker.
Thanks for leading
Linda Bird past George Hamilton
And deliver us from the Kennedys.
Amen, you all.
(P.S. Can't you do something about Sam Houston?)

ALL PURPOSE LIBERAL OR NATIONAL
CATHOLIC REPORTER VERSION

You, who until Leslie Dewart can come up
With something better, we'll call God,
About this oversimplified concept of heaven.
Give up your ancient authoritarianism
And try to be more open, like us.
Bread alone is not enough to cope
With all the varieties of our unrest,
Especially under one species.
We'll try our patient utmost to remain
Within the historical outpost of your domain
(But you might think about meeting us
    halfway).
May all old pastors die off sickly,
and collegiality come most quickly.
End.

Jack and the Giant

(after Graham Greene)

JUAN AWOKE with the taste of mortal sin like ashes in his mouth. He opened one eye and looked at the ceiling, where a blue fly with a gleaming, distended abdomen sat inverted watch beside a jagged crack in the abode. Brown water oozed slowly through the crack, gathered itself reluctantly into globules and splatted down on the earthen floor beyond the foot of Juan's pallet where two lizards were having slippery sex in the mud.

So it was raining still. The cold, driving rain of November which Padre Tómas spoke of in the church: "It is the tears of the Poor Souls in Purgatory which they shed because of the sins of the people of this village."

Juan could hear his mother snoring on her ancient bed in the next room and said a prayer to Saint Jude, patron of hopeless causes, that she would remain asleep until he could get safely away from the house. Not that he really thought that Saint Jude would be disposed to answer such a petition, but he could not face another scene such as he'd had with his mother last night when she discovered that he'd sold the goat for a pack of cigarettes.

It had been a hasty thing to do. They needed money, not cigarettes. But they were American—a pack complete—and Juan felt sure that he could hold out five for himself and still realize as much from the sale of the remaining fifteen as from the scraggly goat whose udder was perpetually dry.

But his mother had not given him a chance to explain. She fell upon him with the broom handle, beating him severely about the head and cursing him for a greedy fool. She tore the cigarettes from his hand, ripped off the top of the package and flung the contents out the window into the rain. Juan rushed out to retrieve them but the beautiful white cylinders were already soaked and disintegrating when he found them so that he had to come back into the house with nothing to show but a few flecks of the excellent tobacco on his fingers. His mother beat him again and sent him off to bed without even half of their one remaining tortilla.

Juan sat up and hurled a sandal at the shameless lizards. Then he lay back again and measured with his hands the dimensions of the great emptiness in his stomach. His mother's snores continued, mounting louder and louder. She is scolding me even yet, he thought, beating me in her sleep, and he tried to shut out the sound.

He would not get up. There was no place to go but out into the rain. He thought of a sunny day in summer when his father was still alive and there had been beans and tacos at almost every meal. There had been a flock of goats then, all fat. Then he thought of the man who had offered him the cigarettes yesterday afternoon.

He had stopped Juan on the road to the village— a huge man, much over six feet in height. He had a wide, thick featured face with bright red lips, which slid back when he spoke to reveal yellow teeth, long and curving, like tusks. He reminded Juan of the devil who lay writhing under the feet of the statute of San Miguel the Archangel in the church.

"I have a taste for meat tonight," he said. "Sell me your goat."

Juan wondered if a man could truly eat an entire goat at one sitting and decided that this one was capable of it. At the thought of meat, Juan felt his stomach begin to rumble and to still it he rolled over, put his face to the pallet and tried to think of nothing. The rain beat down and the lizards resumed their tireless round. Juan dozed off and almost immediately began to dream.

The rain had stopped and a bright sun poured through his window. Juan dressed and went outside to stretch himself in its warmth. But when he went out through the door it was into shade, not sunshine. The shade was cast by an enormous plant which rose from the exact spot where the cigarettes had fallen. Juan could not see the top of the plant because of the huge, broad leaves which hung on every side, but it must be very tall. Immediately, Juan began to climb the plant, moving easily up the thick stalk. The leaves smelled vaguely of tobacco and it was pleasant moving up and up, now in the sun, now in the shade.

Juan climbed until the house was but a tiny speck below him and still he could see no top to the plant. Up and up he went until he could no longer see the house at all and wisps of gray cloud swept past him. Then, just as he was beginning to tire, he saw a cliff which jutted toward the stalk of the plant from the right and seemed to converge with it a point above him. Quickly he climbed to the place where they met and stepped off onto the ground. He was at the edge of a long, broad meadow which sloped upward toward the horizon. In the distance was a single building with a spire. Juan walked quickly toward it. The building appeared to be a church—white and gleaming, a beautiful structure such as he had never seen. Could this be Heaven, Juan wondered? Had he died of hunger and not even known it?

Juan stopped in front of the church. There was a broad set of steps leading up to a pair of massive bronze doors. Juan climbed the steps and wondered whether it would be better manners to knock or simply push open the doors and step inside as one would usually enter a church. He decided it would be best to knock. But even before his hand could grasp the great metal ring of the knocker, the doors parted and Padre Tómas stood between them, glaring out at him.

"Is it possible," he said in his usual baleful voice, "that such a one as you presumes to be admitted here?"

There seemed to be another figure standing in the deep shadow just behind Padre Tómas, but Juan could not see who it was.

"Please, Padre," said Juan, "may I not come in for just a moment?"

"What do you think?" Padre Tómas turned and asked the figure in the shadow.

"Under no circumstances. We cannot admit his sort." Juan started. There was no mistaking his mother's voice.

Padre Tómas turned back to Juan, regarding him with an expression of naked distaste.

"You have heard," he said. "Since you may not come in you must go back down. It will not be quite so pleasant as coming up, I assure you." And with that he pushed the doors tightly shut, almost cutting off Juan's nose.

Juan turned and went slowly down the steps. Truly, there seemed nothing to do but go back down and he started slowly out across the meadow toward the distant cliff. The fact that his mother hated him so deeply did not surprise Juan, but he wondered how she came to be inside the strange church. Had she, too, died of hunger? Juan brooded about this as he walked and so did not at first hear the heavy footsteps behind him. When he did, he whirled about in panic and saw that the church doors had been thrown open and already running toward him in full stride came the huge and villainous-looking man to whom he had traded the goat. He was carrying something in his right hand which looked horribly familiar and when he saw that Juan had seen

him, began to roar obscenities and threats with every step.

Juan did not wait to see what it was that the man was carrying or what it was he wanted with him but turned immediately and began to run for the stalk. Juan had always considered himself to be a very fine runner, faster than most of the village boys, but now his legs seemed hardly to move and he heard the man's footsteps closing in on him. In his terror, Juan almost ran off the edge of the cliff and only at the last second managed to turn and run along it toward the plant. The man shifted course instantly to cut him off. Only by diving headlong through the air, risking everything, did Juan manage to elude the man's outstretched arm.

To Juan's amazement, the man did not try to follow him down the stalk but instead leaned out above him and watched his incredibly slow and clumsy descent. Then with a great laugh that rolled out and down, beating at Juan's ears like the heavy wings of a bird of prey, the man raised his right arm and hurled the object he'd been carrying.

Juan stopped, paralyzed with fear. The object came toward him slowly, turning lazily in the air, straight for his upturned face. It was the severed head of the goat, the eyes wide open and staring reproachfully at Juan with the mouth split and set in a satanic leer.

In the second before it struck him, Juan saw the man lose his balance and fall from the cliff; heard his roar of fear and outrage. Then Juan himself was falling headlong through the clouds. It grew darker and things brushed against him. The air seemed full of writhing, twisting reptile bodies, intertwined, flailing the air with clawed feet. Juan tried to begin a prayer to his guardian angel but could not think of the words. The man appeared beside him and reached for him even as they fell, his yellow teeth gnashing and shredding the red lips in soundless fury. The ground rushed up to meet them. Juan met it with the top of his head, which split into pieces at the impact.

Juan sat up on the pallet. His mother stood over him holding the broom.

"Get up," she said, "or must I give you another. Padre Tómas has been here with important news. The man to whom you sold the goat has been found dead. A bone caught in his throat and choked him. He was an evil man—a murderer with a price on his head. Since it was a bone from our goat which killed him, Padre Tómas—what a saintly man he is—persuaded the authorities that the reward should come to me. Your stupidity has brought us a fortune but do not think on that account that I will forgive you."

Juan got up and looked for his sandals. The lizards lay in the corner, dead of exhaustion. Juan dressed and went outside. The sun was not shining but at least it had stopped raining. Juan supposed that he should go to the church, thank Padre Tómas and offer a candle in thanksgiving. Instead, recalling his dream, he decided he would go to have a look at the dead murderer.

Minutes of an extraordinary meeting of the St. Prometheus Parish Council convened at the special request of the Right Reverend George McMann, pastor and honorary chairman of the Council. All members of the board were present, plus a non-voting attendance of interested parties numbering approximately 680 (janitor's estimate) or virtually the entire registered adult population of the parish. The meeting was called to order at 8:30 p.m. in the school gym-cafeteria complex by Dr. Clive Barnes, D.D.S., council president, who introduced Monsignor McMann as the first, and as it happened, only speaker of the evening.

Our Parish Council Meets Sex Education *or* I Was Furious, Purple

MSGR. McMANN: Well, we all turned out for this one, didn't we? You don't have to be Hans Kung or Karl Rahner to figure out that this isn't Forty Hours Devotion. I haven't seen so many of you in one spot at one time since we played ten-dollar-a-card bingo for that yellow Caddy back in '57. In my seminary days old Father Burke, God rest his tough old soul, used to tell us: "There's nothing like sex or money to bring'em up out of the woodwork." And I was still so wet behind the ears that I didn't know what he meant.

But I didn't come all the way back from Arizona to joke. Any time I interrupt my winter vacation you can bet it's no laughing matter. Next to atheistic Communism, sex is the most disgusting, insidious force at work in the world today. Now I know that a lot of you out there don't take sin very seriously any-more. I know that there are women in this parish who swallow contraceptive pills and then parade up to Communion on Sunday morning like so many lilies of the valley. They've got a million cute little excuses for the confessional—when they bother to confess it at all. The pill regulates this and stabilizes that, and doctor so-and-so says they simply couldn't live without it. But they know and I know that they're taking them because they want to have their cake and eat it too. Disgusting pandering to animal appetites—that's all it is!

No, I can't expect people who laugh and sneer at the teaching of our infallible Holy Father to worry about sex, or Communism, for that matter. And the two are more closely linked than some of you wise-guy liberals out there realize. It wasn't the John Birch Society that introduced sex education for in-nocent little grade school children, I can tell you that. The fact that the Commies have worked their will on the public school system doesn't surprise me in the least. I'm not surprised, either, that now they're trying to infect the last bastion of decency left in this country—our good white Catholic schools. What does surprise and shock me is to see some of our very own sisters and one of my own assistants not only taken in by the plot but working actively to foment it. How far they're actually in-volved in this I haven't been able to determine but if I were them I wouldn't be ordering any return address labels for next year.

I want to stop right here and now and thank Doctor Barnes not just for calling this special meet-ing tonight but for phoning me long distance to let me know what was going on back here. It's getting so a person can't get away for a few weeks without things going to hell on wheels. As I understand it, all the children in the sixth, seventh and eighth grades were to be exposed to a series of films called "The Great Adventure," which is the fancy name some pervert thought up to camouflage some of the fil-thiest sex movies you can imagine. Some people actually wanted to screen those films here tonight "so the parents can decide for themselves," but I can assure you that I'm not going to have that on my conscience or put a lot of innocent people in the direct occasion of serious mortal sin.

You'll just have to take the word of an old and experienced confessor that these films—and there are so-called "correlated reading materials" as well, just as filthy—that this stuff is not kidding around about birds, bees, flowers and storks. No sir and no mam! They pull it right straight from the gutter, the real undiluted stuff—male and female private parts in living color; sperm swimming around fertilizing everything in sight; ovaries discharging right before your very eyes; pictures of a baby being born; pictures of nasty little cells in the very act of dividing. That's the sort of stuff they want to project on our classroom walls, right up there under the crucifix, in full view of the statue of Our Blessed Lady conceived without sin!

Now I know that there are many good souls here tonight and I apologize for having to talk of such disgusting things in front of a mixed audience. In the old days a word to the head of the Holy Name Society would have been sufficient. But now we've got collegiality and co-responsibility and it's not always so pleasant, is it? I can see that many of you are genuinely as shocked as I am. If it affects you that way just think what it would do to the tender souls of our little ones.

But there are some here who think I'm old-fashioned and authoritarian. One mother even went so far as to tell me that she'd rather have her girl shocked than pregnant. Well, you can ask Dr. Barnes and the members of the Parish Council—most of them—and they'll tell you that I'm as open-minded and progressive as they come. I don't know what-all foolishness I've already gone along with in the past ten years from ripping out our $50,000 Italian marble Communion rail to letting the CCD kids invite Jews and Protestants to the parish teen dance. But I will not, I cannot stand still for this. There will be no "Great Adventure" films shown in our parish school. There will be no sex education courses of any kind in my school—ever—period! You can argue and whine and stamp your liberal-hippie feet until they're sore, but it won't change my mind. There will be no further discussion of the matter and there will be no vote taken here tonight.

Now let's all rise and close the meeting with a prayer to St. Thomas Aquinas who drove the harlot from his room with a burning faggot.

All About Paul

JUDGE: State your name, age and occupation.

PLAINTIFF: My name is Cash Delaney, age 54, and I'm editor-in-chief of the publishing firm of Mc-Gullible Hill, New York.

JUDGE: Please tell the court what happened on the afternoon of March 14 last.

PLAINTIFF: Well, it was three o'clock and I'd just gotten back from lunch. I was a little wiffed from three martinis but there was lots to be done so I was irritated when my secretary buzzed to say that there was a peculiar-looking old broad outside who claimed she had a manuscript that I'd cut my throat if I let get away. Now, I've heard that one a thousand times but in this business you never know. Lord, it might have been Anastasia out there, or Amelia Earhart with the saga of her sex-life in Polynesia. So I agreed to see her.

Well, nobody likes to knock old ladies—I mean we've all got aging mothers and aunts—but what came through my office door shouldn't have been allowed out without a sheet over it. Short, dark, lumpy, with knotty legs and long muscular arms. Mercifully, it wore a black veil over its face.

"My name ees Princess Anna Maria Vespuchiossi," it said in a voice that sounded like somebody was murdering a cat in a sewer. "And I have zee hottest book since zee Bible for you." It laid a huge red leather briefcase on my desk and in the process revealed a pair of hairy wrists that could have belonged to King Kong.

"One moment," I said, "I wasn't born yesterday. You're not a woman at all! What do you mean coming in here in drag? Who are you?"

"Ah, so you see through my little disguise," it said, suddenly whisking off the veil and assuming a much deeper but no pleasanter voice. "That is good! It was designed both to protect my identity and to test your keenness. This manuscript cannot be placed in the hands of fools."

"Well, just who the hell *are* you," I shouted glaring at the close-set eyes and heavily-jowled face before me.

"Forswear the profanity if you please," said the new voice, "for I am none other than Nitti Cardinal Gritti, Prince of the Church and personal aide to His Holiness the Pope."

"You'll pardon me, your Eminence," I said, "but I've never heard of you and, under the circumstances, you'll admit that I have reason to doubt that you're telling the truth."

"You are truly a suspicious man," the Cardinal snapped. "The reason you've not heard my name is that I am a Cardinal *in petti,* known only to His Holiness, to a few officials of the Curia and now, to you. I am charged with obtaining a suitable publisher for this manuscript which is nothing less than the personally written autobiography of the Holy Father. Understandably pained and humiliated by the malicious and bloodless image of himself created by the international conspiracy of the world press which is controlled by Masons and Communists, he seeks to rectify those mistaken impressions through

the honest yet extremely colorful account of his life in these precious pages. I've come to you first because your firm is known for its ability to exploit these same minions of the press in order to sell the highest numbers of your books. His Holiness wishes this one to reach every household in the world."

I was, of course, quite staggered. If this Nitti Gritti *in petti* was who he said he was and was handing me the genuine thing it would be the biggest coup of my splendid career.

"You're prepared to provide authentication?" I inquired.

"But naturally," replied the Cardinal opening his red case. "First of all, here is a recent photograph of the Holy Father at work on this self-same manuscript [he produced a photo of the Pope writing at a desk]; next here is a box of earth from the Holy Father's native village of Spumone [he handed me a box containing a handful of rocky soil with the words 'Terra di Spumone' imprinted on the lid]; finally, here is a Papal Blessing made personally to your name and signed by the Holy Father."

The scroll he handed me was on parchment, sealed with red wax and ribbons and hand-lettered to Cash Delaney. It certainly looked authentic and in the face of such overwhelming proof I had no alternative but to presume that I was indeed being presented with the true autobiography of Pope Paul.

"Give me a few days to examine the manuscript, your Eminence," I said, trying hard to suppress the mounting excitement I was experiencing.

"Ah, my dear Cash Delaney," he said, "now it is

my turn to be suspicious. I cannot permit this manuscript out of my sight until we have signed the contract which I have brought with me. The Xerox machine is the devil's own invention and, while you are doubtless a man of sterling integrity, it is always possible that others here may not share that virtue. No, I must insist that you look through the manuscript here and now—and very quickly make your decision." He made a point of fingering a business card which I had no trouble recognizing as belonging to our arch-competitor, Redundant House.

What incredible gall! But, thinking it over, I decided that this was yet another proof that I was really dealing with the Vatican. Quickly I skimmed through the meticulously typed pages. A treasure-trove of ancedotes leapt out: the Pope as a typical fun-loving boy who once got punished for floating his toy boat in a holy water font; the Pope as brilliant young student—and what he did on his summer vacations; as a rising young churchman sent on secret missions of dazzling boldness such as his never-before revealed trip to Peking; his candid impressions of celebrities, including Jackie Onassis. Hundreds of things like that! Obviously this was going to be the bestest seller of all time. Visions of magazine and paperback fees danced before my eyes; I was beginning to cast the movie when I was abruptly brought out of my reverie by the sound of a loud cough.

Cardinal Gritti was smiling a crooked, sardonic little leer. He held out a contract. "All world rights shall be exclusively yours as well as all subsidiary rights; we ask no royalty as such in order that you may hold the price of the book as low as possible so that it may be purchased by the poor and oppressed as well as by the rich; we ask nothing but a mere token payment of $1,000,000 which the Holy Father will use to further his own private charities."

This was too good to be true! I raced through the fine print confirming everything he had said. A gold mine—I'd get the million back on the trade edition alone. Normally I would have called the chairman and probably convened the directors for a deal of this magnitude but the Cardinal was waggling that card again and looking impatient.

"How do I make out the check," I said, signing the contract.

"You are truly a man of decision," said the Cardinal. "I congratulate you. For purposes of discretion the check should be made payable to the name I used upon entry. The Princess Vespuchiossi is my cousin and will deposit the funds in the Vatican Bank in due course. May I suggest that before we go to the bank to have the check certified you make sure the manuscript is placed in your safe."

I didn't think it proper to ask the Cardinal to celebrate the contract with a drink so we parted at the bank and I wandered over to Redundant House to have one in private with their editor, a friendly rival. I could hardly wait to see the look on Fred's face when I dropped my little bomb. Instead, he laughed in my face.

"You didn't buy that hokum papal autobiography, did you? It's the biggest con on the street. Being peddled by a mean-looking little guy who claims to be a Cardinal? He's actually". . . . It was here that I fainted and remember nothing further until I came to in the hospital.

If it please the court, I still can't believe it. Would you like to see my Papal Blessing?

Winnie-the-Pooh

After Flannery O'Connor

AT SUNDOWN the boy, Rufus, who was eight, came out on the porch and sat down on the top step in front of where his grandmother was rocking.

"You come down off Pout Mountain yet?" asked the grandmother. Earlier in the day Rufus's stepmother, Winifred, had caught him smoking a catalpa pod behind the chicken house and beat him with a barrel stave. Rufus hid himself under the house and sulked there, not even coming out for supper.

"She shouldn't oughta have hit me like that," Rufus protested. "If Pap were still alive he'd kick her teeth in for me. Why'd he have to take up with her anyhow? Nothin' but Birmingham trash."

"Don't let it take you so hard," said the grandmother, who had asked the same question of herself. "Suppose I tell you a story before we go to bed? It might ease your spirit."

"It won't ease my spirit none if it's about any of them talkin' animals which is really a fairy prince that's been bushwhacked by some witch. You must have told me a hundert of them. Don't you know any stories where somebody ends up trompin' their stepmother in the face?"

"No," said the grandmother, "but I do know a story about a boy and a bear."

"What was the boy's name," Rufus asked, intrigued in spite of himself.

"His name was C. R. and he was about your age or a little younger and he lived in a cabin in the piney woods just about like this one."

"What was C. R. the short of?" asked Rufus.

"Christopher Robin," said the grandmother.

"I can see why he wanted people to call him C. R., all right," said Rufus. "What happened about the bear?"

"If you'll keep shut for a spell, I'll tell you," said the grandmother. "It begins when C. R. was out in the woods one day, hunting squirrels with a .22, when he comes across this bear sittin' alongside a cyprus stump. It wasn't a big bear so C. R. figured he'd just have a shot at him from a far piece and take off runnin' in case he missed a mortal wound."

"What color was the bear?" Rufus demanded.

"What difference does that make?" the grandmother replied. "I thought you wanted this story to move along."

"Everything makes a difference," said Rufus. "I got to know what color was the bear."

"Well," said the grandmother, looking hard at the back of Rufus's scrawny neck where the top end of a welt still showed, "it wasn't black nor brown nor any of your regular bear colors. I'd say it was a kind of a washed-out carrot color, about the shade of your stepmother's hair."

"Good," said Rufus, "now tell me about how he shot it in the gut."

"Hold on there, Mister," said the grandmother. "This is my story and I'll say what happened next if it's all the same to you. As a matter of fact, C. R. didn't fire on the bear at all, on account of when he was just fixin' to pull the trigger the bear ups and says, 'Don't shoot!' "

"I knew it," said Rufus. "A talkin' bear. I'll bet he was really a fairy prince all along. You only got one string on your banjo, like I said."

"You're just like your pap when he was a boy," said the grandmother. "Full of sass and vinegar. Think you know how many beans is in the bag afore you count them." She gave Rufus a sharp poke in the ribs with her cane.

"The bear could talk all right, because this here was a 'chanted forest," she continued, "but it weren't no fairy prince. It told C. R. its name was Pooh, and that if he didn't shoot, it'd show him where lots of varmits lived that he could shoot."

"Pooh?" said Rufus. "That ain't no kind of name for a bear. You can't even tell if it's a him or a her."

"That's right, you can't," said the grandmother, who went right on with the story. "C. R. figured he might as well go along with the bear as he could shoot it any time he wanted and still get a pack of other game as well.

"First off, the bear takes him to a hole in the side of a hill. 'Come out here for a minute, Rabbit!' yells the bear. And sure enough a rabbit pokes his head out long enough for C. R. to blast him.

" 'That's one,' says the bear and leads C. R. off to a clearing where this funny little wild donkey and a baby pig is walkin' round in a circle together like they was talkin' over something mighty serious. C. R. kneels down and gets them both, neat as you please. 'That's two and three,' says the bear."

"You really 'spect me to swallow that?" said Rufus, spitting to show what he thought of the story so far.

The grandmother raised her cane again.

"Go ahead," Rufus said, "I ain't sick to my stomach yet."

"Next the bear takes C. R. to a big tree with a rope hanging down out of it. 'When I pull this here rope you be ready to shoot,' says the bear. He yanks on the rope and right away an owl comes out of a knothole and sits there on a limb blinkin' and turnin' his head till C. R. lines one up into his gizzard.

" 'That's four and a good shot, I don't mind tellin' you,' says the bear."

"Anybody that can't knock a hoot-owl out of a tree ought to have his gun took away," Rufus said under his breath.

"Just then C. R. hears a terrible roar and turns round to see a tiger bearin' down on him like the morning freight. 'You're on your own,' says the bear, duckin' behind the tree.

"Now C. R. weren't countin' on running into no tigers and it gave him a mean start. But he wasn't no boy to lose his head so he throws up the .22 and shoots."

"Ain't no .22 made gonna stop no tiger," said Rufus, disgusted.

"Boy," said the grandmother, "what you don't know could fill a silo. That bullet went smack down the tiger's throat and busted his spleen. Ever'body who's been to a Tar Sam movie in Birmingham knows that's the only place to jab a tiger. He was dead afore he hit the ground."

"It was a mighty lucky shot then," said Rufus, more impressed than he cared to admit.

"That's just what the bear said when he came out from behind the tree," the grandmother went on. " 'Five must be your lucky number,' he told C. R. and led him off into the woods again, farther than C. R.'d ever been before, to where there was a little house."

"Who lived there?" asked Rufus, forgetting himself.

"You got the patience of a bitch in heat, ain't you?" said the grandmother. "Only they got better manners." She was pleased, all the same, that Rufus took such an interest in her story.

"It turned out it was the bear's house. It bein' able to talk and all you don't s'pose it'd be livin' in some cave, did you?"

"A course not," said Rufus.

"And hoppin' around in front of the house was two of the strangest lookin' critters that C. R. had ever seen—a big un and a little un—with long tails and terrible big bottom feet. They looked like giant rats, only they sat up on their hind legs and covered about a rod ever'time they took a jump.

" 'Them is kangaroos,' the bear told C. R., 'and you better shoot 'em fast else they'll kick the bejesus out of you.' Well, C. R. he didn't like their looks much so he gets the big one first and then the little one—right in the middle of a hop.

" 'That's six and seven,' says the bear . . ."

"What's all this fool countin' for," Rufus interrupted again. "Sounds to me like you just can't think a nothin' else for the bear to say."

"It's a good thing for you that you don't have no school to go to," said the grandmother triumphantly, "cause they'd throw you back the first day for not bein' able to see the book in front of your nose. How many shots does that old .22 of your pap's hold?"

"Seven," said Rufus, realizing that he'd let his grandmother lead him into a trap.

"That's right," she said. "And so did C. R.'s. And that bear, Pooh, who was smarter'n you and C. R. put together, he knew it too.

" 'Now you've cut it, boy,' says the bear to C. R. 'You're clean out of bullets and I'm goin' to have you for lunch. I'm obliged to you for shootin' all them other pests for me and also for comin' right along to my house so nice like. I hates to drag my food a long way.' And with that he jumps at C. R. and tries to get a hold on his throat."

Rufus could stand it no longer. "You goin' to let that runty carrot-colored bear get the best of him?" he shouted. "It's a mighty poor kind of story if you do."

"Got you worried, ain't I?" cackled the grandmother. "As it happened, old C. R. was just a might too fast for the bear. He just took a little step to the side and let the bear sail by him and fall flat on its face. Then C. R. takes the rifle by the barrel and beats the bear over the head with the butt till it was stone cold dead."

"That's more like it," said Rufus, pleased. "That's the best story you've ever told."

The grandmother was just-about to ask Rufus if he felt like eating a bite of supper now when she was brought up short by a shout from inside the cabin.

"Can't you two stop that eternal caterwaulin' out there?" It was Rufus's stepmother calling from her bed. "My head's like to split it aches so bad and I don't aim to stand for all that racket. This here is my house now and don't neither of you forget it!"

"Don't you fret yourself none, Winifred," the grandmother called back, "Rufus and me was just fixin' to go to bed."

To Rufus, in a much lower tone of voice she said, "Fancy that, she's got a headache now. Ain't that a pity?"

"That's eight," said Rufus, smiling for the first time all day.

How Green Was My Fairway

(The Real Father Urban Stands Up)

Rev. John Kelleher
Clementine Fathers
St. Clement's Hill
Deusterhaus, Minnesota

Dear Jack,

This is a letter I was hoping I wouldn't have to write. Not that I wasn't going to drop you a line in a few days, anyway, but I didn't want it to be like this, under duress. I won't try to kid you, I've known I'd have some explaining to do ever since September when I ran across an ad announcing publication of a novel called—Hang on to your nine-iron!—*Morte D'Urban* by an author named J. F. Powers. In spite of the title I wouldn't have given it a second thought if it hadn't been for the author's name. Remember how you told me you felt when you first heard about Pearl Harbor—a combination of blind rage and nausea. Well that's how I felt when I read that ad, only more so, since I didn't know how bad the damage was going to be.

All I knew was that I had spent an evening a couple of years back with a character named Jim Powers (I still haven't found out what the "F" stands for; probably Freemason) and that now here was a novel "about a priest who tried to beat the world at its own game," which had my name mixed up in the title. Right then, as I told the Provincial (I put off telling him as long as I could in the hope that the book would drop out of sight before he got wind of it—it's a first novel—but *Time* had to review it and, as we all know from reading his column in *The Clementine*, the Provincial definitely reads *Time*: "Too little and too lightly regarded by most Catholics, the Holy Season of Advent next week will begin without most of them even being aware of the fact."), I knew I had been sold down the river by one of the smoothest con-men to don the habit since Richelieu. Obviously, I don't mean Powers; you don't blame the bullet for the hole in your back. I don't like to tie name tags to my black tales, but since you and Wilf and almost everybody else in the Order are involved (you're one of the main characters, by the way) you've got a right to know who fingered you. None other than that most frequent user of the Hill's fairways, our mutual friend, Father Feld.

Ever since the weekend I took him for three

straight rounds (his putting was off, he said, because he'd burned his right palm filling a red hot censer at Forty Hours Devotion earlier in the week) I knew I wasn't heading up his list of favorite people. But I guess I really poured salt on a boil when I kidded him about the Christian Family Movement one day during the time I was pinch-hitting at St. Monica's. A lot of the bigger bucks in the diocese had come around to say goodbye to Phil (the Pastor) and Monsignor Renton before they left on vacation, Feld among them. We were all sitting around sampling some of the liquid assets one of the more thoughtful parishioners had sent over in a plain brown wicker hamper ("Bon Voyage to a real swell Pastor"), talking a little shop. Feld's palm must still have been bothering him a lot, because he kept it wrapped around a cold glass practically continuously. It wasn't long before he got expansive and told how he was the one who had really gotten CFM off the ground in the Diocese, more or less over the Bishop's dead body.

I would have let it go, but somebody who should have known better had dragged along a matched pair of first assignment curates, still pale and liberal from the seminary, and they sat there listening to Feld as if he had been dictating *Rerum Novarum* on the spot, so I had to throw a harpoon. It had been a long hard week taking over the keys to Phil's kingdom, and I had shaken hands with Johnny Walker a few times myself, so it was a pretty blunt instrument I used; something about the Bishop's having told me that the only way he could ever manage to get anything new started in the Diocese was to act like he was dead set against it.

If looks could keep you in Purgatory, the one Feld gave me would have paid my dues for a century or two, and seeing that I'd gotten onto his green, I used my best pulpit voice to ask Monsignor Renton if he'd heard how the little boy in religion class had defined CFM. (You've heard that one: "Can't Find Mamma—she's gone to a meeting.") Feld was still too conscious of his new-found disciples to blow up. He gave me a tight little smile, the kind missionaries say you can see on the face of a cobra just before it strikes, and left.

Well, aside from giving myself a few penalty strokes for lack of charity, I didn't give the matter another thought. I should have, especially when Feld called up about two weeks later with his mouth full of honey and told me that he thought he was on to something really big in the way of a publicity break for the Order. He had run into an old college friend of his, a free-lance writer who regularly had his stuff published in the big magazines. He said they'd gotten to talking about new developments in the Diocese and that he had told his friend all about the Clementines coming in and starting a retreat house and what a wonderful thing the Hill could develop into, *and* that his friend had immediately wondered if there might not be a good story in it.

That hooked me, of course, since Feld knew that right then I would have stood on my head for even a paragraph in the Deusterhaus *Daily Dairyman* and he was larding every sentence with names like *Post, Life* and *Look*. He got to toying with me at the end, wondering if, just as a personal favor to him, I could spare a few hours to talk to his friend that evening? You've got to be really sure of yourself to lay on the expensive spread like that. He knew I'd have made time for his friend during my own mother's canonization, if need be. Even then he couldn't stop, but fell all over himself thanking me, and all the while I kept right on swimming for the deep water, not even feeling the plug in my mouth.

"Friend," of course, turned out to be good old Jim Powers and I still can't do more than regret that there are men in the world who have to make their living the way he does. I understand he has a big family and I guess it's less risky than blackmail and cleaner than digging up cadavers. I won't bore you with the details of how I played into his hands that

night; suffice it to say that given Powers' peculiar talents ("We've got to get behind the scenes, Father"), I couldn't have done more for his novel if I had handed it to him, page at a time, typed double-space and all ready to go.

Feld came by to collect him a little after midnight, looking as pleased with himself as if he'd just converted Russia single-handedly. We all had a nightcap with both of them having an increasingly hard time keeping their faces straight (I thought they were just happy about a job well done; which, of course, they were). Really, looking back at the whole thing, I think the hardest thing to swallow (the book itself still doesn't seem real to me) is the memory of that farewell scene on the front porch of St. Monica's Rectory. I clasped Powers' hand in both of mine and told him that St. Clement was probably even then polishing up a crown for him; Feld, I actually embraced, and asked what I had ever done to deserve such a kindness. It was stickier than the ending of *Goodbye, Mr. Chips!* I don't know how they did it, but they both managed to make it off the porch and into Feld's car without breaking up.

That's all I heard about it (thank God, I was at least able to restrain myself from asking Feld if he'd heard which magazine would be carrying the article) until I saw that ad in September. Two days

later I got a copy of the book in the mail with a little
inscription scrawled on the flyleaf:

> Abou Ben Urban,
> May his drive decrease,
> Awoke one day
> From a deep dream . . .
> —from all the gang at CFM
>   (Cry For Mercy)

For a few days after he read the book, the Provincial didn't say anything; in fact, he hardly moved.
Then he called me in and asked if I thought, (1)
Was there any chance at all of getting the thing put
on the Index, fast? and (2) Did Canon Law permit
a religious order to sue for libel? I told him "No" on
both counts and that there was nothing we could do
but grin and bear it in the true spirit of Christian
humility.

I sincerely hope that you and Wilf will be able to
look at it the same way, though I don't think it
would hurt to go down to the locker room ("We
don't need locks here at St. Clement's Hill, men")
and take Father Feld's new set of Arnold Palmer
woods out to the lake and see if they will float. It
seems the very least we could do, considering that
we've already been hit on both cheeks.

> As ever,
> (Rev.) Urban Roche

Life with Father

Dear Ann Blanders:

Recently I left the Roman Catholic priesthood to marry a widow with five children. A number of my former colleagues joined the bishop in warning me that I was making a stupid mistake and that any forty-six-year-old bachelor, let alone one who had been a priest and pastor, would have enormous difficulties adjusting to family life. Well, they were wrong, and I hope you'll publish this letter for the benefit of all those disenchanted priests who've let the kill-joy prophets of doom talk them out of marrying.

In the beginning, I'll admit, it was a trifle difficult. Women, as you know, are curious, prideful creatures not much good at reasoning things through or tackling problems in a practical, business-like way. My wife, for instance, had no money sense at all. She took it for granted that she would have ready access to my income through a joint checking account, charge cards and a non-accountable petty-cash fund. She even demanded to know how much I made in my new job as manager of the large construction firm which hired me as soon as I let my availability be known. (That's another song-and-dance my former priest friends gave me—that a pastor isn't qualified for a comparable job in the secular world.) It didn't take me long to explain the voucher and centralized purchasing system I've used with such singular success over the years. A bill without a purchase order approved by me means a trip back to the store, I can tell you that!

And the poor dear had some notion that we'd be taking vacations together, as a family! The places in Florida where I stay won't even take curates, let alone children and dogs. I had to explain that there simply wouldn't be any point in taking a vacation *with* your family. The whole point is to get away from day-to-day problems. Why, I'd just as soon take along a bishop! She took this badly for a while, I must say, but felt considerably better when I gave her Wednesday afternoons off with the use of the car until five-thirty.

She also failed to understand why my mother and my former housekeeper had to move in with us after the honeymoon. A man's relationship with his mother is scared, of course, and now that I don't have to live apart from her anymore I was simply fulfilling the natural law by keeping her close to me where she belongs. The housekeeper knows how I like my food prepared and my pajamas ironed. I wouldn't dream of throwing my always delicate digestion open to the ravages of the wanton succession of hot dogs and hamburgers which my wife prepares for the children.

We have separate rooms, of course. Sex is all well and good and I enjoy it as much as the next man. But after a simple time and motion study it was obvious that it occupies a tiny fraction of a married couple's time. Meanwhile, there's no reason to spoil a restful night's sleep. It's really not terribly healthy to pass a complete night in close proximity to another human being. Still, spontaneity in these matters is terribly important—one can't simply set a schedule and follow it inflexibly. I solved the problem quite neatly, I think, by installing some leftover confessional lights outside our respective bedroom doors. One light on is a question; two lights on, consensus.

The much-dreaded chaos of life with five children was quite easily managed. My regular bulletin is issued every Sunday morning (*The Family Chimes,* I call it) and lists everything from meals to bath times. The children submit their scheduled activities as well as special requests for parties, dates, transportation, etc., to me by Wednesday evening. All approved events are then scheduled chronologically and published. If it's not published they can assume that permission has been withheld. No exceptions are ever made, of course. *The Chimes* also lists the hours for the regularly weekly conference I grant to each child. It has solved all our problems quite handily. My only concern at the moment is with selling advertising spots on the back cover to local merchants. They'll come around in time.

There's a great deal more I could tell you, but by now the point should be obvious: marriage and family life present no problems to the former priest that can't be solved by reason, sound management and a firm pastoral hand. The best endorsement of my methods I can offer comes from my wife who is understandably happy with the way things have worked out. If she's told me once, she's told me a thousand times: "You're just too much, you know that don't you!"

A satisfied Former Celibate

109

Did Jesus take the summer off? You can bet your peak experience he didn't! Be a full-time Christian by attending one or more of the summer workshops described below and blast your relevancy factor out the top of the tube.

Suddenly This Summer

SISTER JOAN'S TRANSACTIONAL DYNAMICS AND SKYDIVING FORUM

In the rolling hills and turbulent skies of beautiful southern Kansas members learn to relate under stress conditions. Says Sister Joan (veteran of 479 free falls): "Anyone can hack it on the ground, but can you trust your brother to pull your rip at 9,000 feet while your hands are tied?" Odd weekends starting mid-June. Blue Cross mandatory. Box 40, Squash Center, Kansas.

HOW DOES YOUR SPIRITUAL GARDEN GROW?

Turn those cockleshells to silver bells at Marydell Farm's summer workshop on Christian Passivity which employs the unique "Vegetable Stassis Method" pioneered by Greta Fallow during the great 17th-century Hungarian onion blight. On June 1 each participant will be given a seed to plant and nurture (no chemical fertilizers). For the rest of the summer you contemplate its growth and eat only the kind of vegetable it turns out to be. Watch your animal appetites disappear completely. One credit in theology and two in biology. Box 3, Del Monte, California.

COMPLETE A SENTENCE . . .

for an oppressed prisoner in a Federal Pen . . .
unique program allows you to serve the remaining
time in place of some unfortunate victim of society's
thirst for vengeance. Volunteers can choose from a
wide range of times from three months to life . . .
experience the inequities of prison at first hand . . .
live with convicted murderers, kidnappers, rapists
and hijackers. The man you free will write you once
a week for the duration. Throw inquiries over the
south wall of San Quentin between 1 and 3 A.M. on
Tuesdays (watch out for the dogs).

BEAT THE DEVIL . . .

at his own game. . . . Pope Paul has warned that
Christians are failing to take Satan seriously . . .
learn the inner workings of covens, the Black Mass,
possession, etc. . . . Four weeks of sheer hell begins
with advance screening of *The Exorcist* and works
up progressively to actual calling up of Lucifer. No
crucifixes or Holy Water, please! Send first-born
child or the tops of three virgins together with your
application to Box 999, Hot Springs, Ga.

WORKSHOP ON PASTORAL PAINTING

One week (or longer if need be) beginning July 3.
Participants will be provided with brush, paint and
ladder and a clear-cut objective as to which area
of house they must cover during the course. Rare
opportunity for meditation on the color white and
the purgation of honest toil. Write: Thomas Sawyer,
Hannibal, Mo.

KNOW THYSELF!

Designed expressly for the Christian whose preoc-
cupation with loving others has blinded him or her
to the splendors of his or her own body. Twelve
lectures beginning May 26, all delivered by the
eminent chiropractor and phrenologist Dr. Murray
("Hands") Holdbinder: "The Inner Ear," "Meet
Your Nostrils," "Those Vicious Vertebrae," "Of
Cuticles and Callouses," "Hands across the Knee,"
"It's Deeper Than You Think," "Mysteries of the
Armpit," "Navigating the Navel," "Don't Be
Ashamed of Your Elbow," "Groin and Bear It,"
"Sitting Pretty," and "How to Take a Shower
Alone." Box 711, Fastbuck, Pa.

THE WORKSHOP GOER'S WORKSHOP

Three-week cram session on how to attend workshops of all descriptions. Explains key terms and
postures . . . what to say when complete strangers
want to touch your body. . . . twelve ways to avoid
exchanging the kiss of peace . . . how to survive the
lousy food . . . what to wear at outdoor song fests,
. . . how to be sure of getting equal time in the bathroom. . . . how to construct a surefire emergency
lock for your room and luggage. . . . four ways to
kill bedbugs. . . . 63 relevant responses to meaningful questions. . . . how to sneak liquor into retreats.
. . . thousands of other essential items for survival
and comfort. Begins June 1, Bear Island Maine—
bring sleeping bag, Fritos and mosquito net.